How Colour Influences
What We Buy, Make and Feel

Colour hunting

Frame Publishers

Contents

Wellbeing

Colour Facts

Introduction

'There are painters who transform the sun into a yellow spot, but there are others who, thanks to their art and intelligence, transform a yellow spot into the sun.'

Pablo Picasso

Without colour, life would be an ongoing journey in black, white and shades of grey. Imagine endless decades without lush green meadows, seductive fire-engine-red lips, mesmerizing ultramarine canvases and fields of cheerful yellow sunflowers. Although we are aware of the important role that colour plays in our lives, what remains a mystery to many of us is the impact that colour has on our behaviour, environment and wellbeing.

For millennia, artists and designers have utilized colour to express ideas and emotions in everything from the frescoes and textiles of ancient civilizations to the *haute couture* and digitally created architecture of today. Some delve deeper beneath the surface than others, as Picasso suggests, to elevate colour to a whole new level. In our hunt for colour, in all its guises and complexity, we explored the very depths of the subject.

In compiling this publication, we considered the many facets and functions of colour, while repeatedly questioning its influence on us and on humans in general. What is it about colour that attracts us when used in a certain way and repulses us under different circumstances? What prompts us to buy a shiny silver car rather than one that is yellow or pink? What's behind our preference for laundry products packaged in blue and organic products wrapped in green? Why does a black tomato look less appetizing than its red ancestor? In other words, how does colour affect what we buy, make and feel?

The in-depth articles and interviews in this book examine the role of colour in commercial projects and artistic concepts and analyse its impact on wellbeing. The first chapter, 'Commerce', looks at colour as a selling tool, casts a light on colour trends and dissects the use of colour in branding messages. The following chapter, 'Aesthetics', offers an insight into the conceptual use of colour, as well as the challenges and techniques entailed when applying colour to a wide range of materials. Our mood responds to the colours around us, even though the underlying cause of this phenomenon may be less than crystal clear. The relationship between body, mind and colour forms the focus of the third chapter, 'Wellbeing'. Facts about colour interspersed throughout the book trace what colour has meant to people and cultures down through the ages in every part of the world.

Initially, bright colours grab our attention and soft shades calm the nerves, but you are about to discover that colour has the power to do far more than that. Although the projects featured here have different outcomes, what they share is an unwavering commitment to pushing the boundaries of colour. We set out on a hunt, broadened our horizons and unearthed the immense potential of colour. When your eyes are open to every nuance, tone, tint and shade, the possibilities are truly infinite.

Hanneke Kamphuis, Hedwig van Onna and Jeanne Tan

Chapter One

Colour & Commerce

Branding

Sexy red, loyal blue, pure White

Large international corporations take a great deal of time arriving at the appropriate colours for their corporate identities. And even for smaller businesses selecting the proper colours is critical for creating a strong brand image.

Author **Leatrice Eiseman**
Photography **Anne Dokter and Frank Visser**

Commerce

Red is a virtually un-ignorable colour; not unexpectedly, the brightest reds make the boldest statements

Experts tell us that we are living in a highly visual society. As a method of coping, consumers of all ages look for visual stimulation. With about 80 per cent of human experience filtered through the eyes, visual cues are vital in getting a message across. Of course, the first challenge is to grab the eye, and nothing does that better than the thoughtful use of colour.

Colour is the most powerful communication tool, even more important than shape or explanatory words. It has the power to differentiate a brand from its competition, sending nonverbal messages with, in many cases, a subliminal effect that affects the way that consumers perceive the brand.

Developing the brand

The development of a 'brand' is effective because a brand directs attention, creates associations and causes people to remember images connected to a service or product. Branding is vital in advertising; brands give products a name and a distinct identity. The brand name Hermès or Nikon may be just as well known as the bag or camera it represents. Brands are recognized by name, quality, reputation – and often by colour. Communications giant Orange has a well-established image linked to a shade of high-visibility orange that speaks of making connections. The forward swing of the Coca-Cola logo is associated with high energy and exuberance.

In thinking about the selection of a colour to represent a brand, it's important to consider the psychological message and meaning of the colour, and how it will broadcast the meaning and image of the company. Studying the competition is also vital; using the same colours as those used by close competitors could be perceived as unoriginal. If the product is to appear on a shelf next to its rivals, it is even more important to have a different palette. Trends should also be taken into consideration. A company does not want its product to appear dated soon after it's launched. In dealing with colour and branding for different media – print, web, billboards – consistency is key. Colours must be the same across all platforms and should be differentiated only within a brand category.

Consumer response to colour can remain fairly constant, change considerably or simply evolve. In preparation for my book, *Color: Messages and Meanings*, updated colour-word association studies were conducted. Each participant was given a specific colour and asked to respond to it on a visceral level, to say the first word or phrase that came to mind. With these reactions, we compiled an emotional response to colour, as well as up-to-date guidelines and the most effective colour combinations, based on our knowledge of specific mixes of colour and how they can suggest moods and convey messages. Certain colours cross cultural boundaries better than others; a good example is red, which radiates positivity in most parts of the world. Coca-Cola, for one, uses red packaging internationally.

Shout it out: red and pink

Starting with red: consumer reactions to this colour remain fairly constant. Throughout history, it has been the colour of enticing, appetite-arousing, ripened fruits and delicious foods that sustain our very existence. It is a virtually un-ignorable colour, which registers without fail even at the farthest edge of our peripheral vision. As studies done at the London School of Economics tell us, the human visual system was shaped eons ago by the colours of many plants and animals: think red, in particular, against the green backdrop of nature.

Word-association studies invariably show that red is perceived as the most sensual of all colours, and, as the saying goes, 'sex sells'. Not unexpectedly, the brightest reds make the boldest statements. Whether expressing danger, celebration, love or passion, lipstick reds, scarlet and crimson will not be ignored. These are the reds that literally, physiologically, 'get the blood up' and arouse the strongest emotion, which is precisely why red was chosen as the symbolic colour for Bono's PRODUCT (RED) effort to raise money for the eradication of AIDS in Africa.

Similarly, vibrant pinks capture some of the same essence of the red that spawns them. Intensely theatrical, they radiate high energy, exerting a youthful and sensual force. When red seems a bit cliché or is in need of a more playful or youthful attitude, hot pinks serve as an excellent stand-in. Lighter pinks and roses carry the connotation of flowers or confections, things sweetly scented and sweet tasting, creating an effect in which sight, taste and scent converge. Like Bono's (RED) campaign, pink has become symbolic of certain social issues and movements, transcending the realm of trends and gaining importance by representing, for example, breast-cancer awareness. A word of caution: it is important to know your customer, as some female consumers, particularly those in their 30s and older, object to a stereotypic use of pink.

The expectation that deeper wine colours will be more expensive than brighter shades can be used to advantage in a marketplace that promotes a world of luxury. Inevitably connected to the 'good life', the former are thought of as elegant, cultivated, rich and refined. Warm reds, associated with the earth and evoking thoughts of sunny countryside settings, can benefit from a bit of exotic interplay with other warm colours, such as hotter pinks and purples.

Visibility and vitality: orange and yellow

There was literally no word for 'orange' in Europe until the fruit arrived from the world's more tropical regions. Oranges became known as the fruit of the gods, of emperors and aristocrats, ultimately gaining symbolic importance in Renaissance paintings. More recent times have seen the popularity of the colour orange plummet among the elite as it was adopted for use in fast-food restaurants. The '90s saw a rebirth of →

orange in the fashion world and, because of global exposure via the Web, a more widespread use of the colour in other cultures. At the same time, consumer products have experienced an explosion of more vibrant colours in general, including orange. The introduction of orange into industrial design in the late '90s did not go unnoticed by Apple's iMac and others: in the world of computers, colour had never been used like this before.

Closely related to red, its 'mother' hue, vibrant orange is a very physical, high-visibility colour that seems to be in constant motion, always moving on and out. But its connection to sunny yellow also makes orange appear to be friendlier and more approachable than red. Orange is a gregarious, fun-loving hue and a great favourite with children, especially as they become more fascinated by secondary colours, which usually occurs from the ages of three to six. The lighter and less-intense orangey tones are perceived as warm and welcoming. They imbue products and packaging with sensory qualities: the customer smells a sweet scent, feels a soft touch, experiences a warm taste and has a pleasurable visual experience.

Invariably connected with the sun, yellow sparkles with heat, vitality, energy. This is the colour that best expresses the essence of light, while also suggesting an intellectual energy, curiosity and need for enlightenment: the ability to see all things more clearly, literally and philosophically. As one of the more important colours in human development, yellow attracts the infant's eye. This is because of the physiological maturation level that allows babies to see bold primary colours before the more nuanced shades. When children are old enough to draw, yellow is the colour that toddlers choose to embellish the upper-right or upper-left side of the paper with a big yellow sun. (Experts say it depends on their right- or left-hand proclivities.) Yellow is the colour of highest visibility, and yellows that are pure, bright and vibrant are the easiest for the human eye to see. This is the colour that heightens awareness and creates clarity. The combination of yellow and all-powerful black is even more attention-demanding (as exemplified by the markings of wasps and New York City taxis).

The softer, more golden shades of yellow generate thoughts of pleasant relaxation and contentment: a good example is comfort food. Times of stress see an increase in the sale of yellow foods, as people revert to childhood comfort foods such as custard and macaroni and cheese.

Earthiness with an indulgent edge: brown

From time immemorial, brown has been identified with the earth and with the diligence it takes to work the land. The wholesomeness and naturalness that is attached to the brown family has been used to great advantage by the food and beverage industry, especially by the manufacturers of coffee and chocolate. The fashionable cachet →

Times of stress see an increase in the sale of yellow foods

currently associated with delicious shades of coffee and chocolate has spread into all areas of design. Certainly chocolate and coffee brown have been around for years, but now they boast an unprecedentedly luxurious edge.

Integrity and loyalty: blue

Long linked to the serenity of a clear blue sky, the light, medium and deep blues summon a feeling of respite and introspection – a quiet, cool permanence. The human mind embraces the concept of blue as tranquil and constant, and translates it into a symbolic image of dependability and loyalty. Obviously, this works well, as it inspires a remarkable sense of dedication in the consumer. Blue is the number-one choice for use in corporate branding and identification. The constant challenge of such pervasive use of the colour is to keep it looking fresh and not hackneyed. If the essential message begs for a true-blue image that speaks of integrity, look for an innovative combination that features a dominant shade of blue. From the Greek *electros*, meaning 'gleaming, shiny and brilliant', comes the range of electric blues that defy the typically cool message of the blue family. Ironically, the hottest stars burn a radiantly intense blue, as do the hottest gas flames.

Health and environment: green

An abundance of green indicates the proximity of water, a resource vital to human survival. As a result, humans respond on a very visceral level to the reassuring presence of green. With a multitude of greens so plentiful in the surrounding world, the human eye literally sees more green than any other colour – and green can convey many moods. A majority of people see green as symbolic of nature and new beginnings, as green refreshes and restores, while reaffirming the unchanging, annual repetition of seasons. Leafy greens equate to newness, youth and growth. Various greens identify vegetables or fruits: organic, fresh, healthy and so important in today's world. Green (as in green tea) is simply good for you, enhancing your life, making you more vital and alleviating stress. The 21st century has been deemed the 'green century', as green symbolically represents the pressing need to make the planet a healthier place.

Today, there is a benevolent aspect to yellow-green, represented in particular by the lovable green characters in children's stories (think *Shrek*) that are prolonging the shelf life of yellow-green in kids' markets.

Studies show that greens with an undertone of blue are among the more popular colours. Teal, for example, is a thoughtful colour that exudes confidence. Although more elegant than an ordinary green or blue, teal embraces the symbolic qualities of both. It is a tasteful colour, often preferred by those who appreciate sophisticated styling, and a rather 'upscale' shade that cannot be described as 'ordinary'.

The uniqueness factor: purple

Purple has its very own distinctive personality; it can define many moods. Depending on the undertones of the shade and its positioning in combinations, purple can be exciting and energizing or mysterious and somewhat mystical. The blue-purples have been used to express certain heavenly, transcendental or spiritual properties, taking awareness to a higher level of thought, related to the cosmos. Purple flowers and foods are more distinctive in appearance or taste than most and support the uniqueness of the hue. Think aubergine, the elegant French word for eggplant – definitely an acquired taste. The 'uniqueness factor' is precisely the reason why I selected purple for one of my clients, the Schick Quattro razor. The exclusivity concept once attached to purple is lost on today's younger generation, however, whose members rarely think in terms of royalty. Young people more often think about purple as the colour of sports equipment or sportswear.

Lavenders, long associated with ageing and femininity, are more transgender nowadays and are used by all ages. Like its cousins in the rose family, lavender is seen as lightweight, sweetly scented and sweet tasting.

Essentials: black, white and neutral

Neutral shades – grey, beige, taupe and off- →

Blue is the number-one choice for use in corporate branding and identity

K
共 撰
ノンステープル

white – speak of longevity. They are symbolic colours accompanying the current move towards sustainable resources, such as natural fibres and recycled paper products.

Strange as it may seem, white is a colour. Pure white is highly visible to the human eye; because of its clarity, it is viewed as brilliant. White always has been and always will be the ultimate representative of purity and cleansing.

And then there's black, the quintessential colour of luxury and power – including 'staying power'. No other hue is as empowering and as sophisticated as black. Think of caviar and the popularity of black diamonds in today's world.

Regarding black and white, many old concepts of 'funerary' colours have faded. More and more, black is being seen as sophisticated, elegant and classic – in all cultures – rather than being relegated to thoughts of death and funerals. Even young Asian brides are wearing white gowns at their weddings, and China Airlines now has a largely white plane. Not long ago, white would have been taboo for any product made for the Chinese market, owing to its association with death. People across the globe with access to the Web and/or TV are far more aware of changes in cultural customs and traditions – and are showing a willingness to adapt to the new.

The combination of yellow and all-powerful black demands attention: think wasps and NYC taxis

Using colour combinations to reach consumers

Obviously, colours are rarely used in isolation. Specific combinations of colour can impart a particular theme that the consumer will link immediately to the brand in question. In two of my books, *The Pantone Guide to Communicating with Color* and *Color: Messages and Meanings*, I explain the importance of using specific colour combinations to enhance an idea or impart a message.

A good example is the choice of a colour family for the design of a label or the creation of a brand image when the product is a robust, deep-red, vintage wine. Certain colours get the message across instantly. The palette should speak quite literally of good taste. Colour variations should be both tasty and tasteful: rich chocolate browns, full-bodied burgundies, shades of claret, sparkling golden sauternes or chardonnays, plum purples, grape and berry reds, all juxtaposed with vineyard greens – the result is a visual feast for the eyes.

If a client asks for a group of colours to promote a new line of fragrances, sensuality might very well play into the final choices. A tantalizing palette that teases all appetites would be one of spicy reds, hot purples, succulent oranges, shocking pinks and tangy Dijon-mustard shades, which could be teamed with a potent black backdrop for added drama. This is not a project suitable for pale tones, which would conjure an inappropriate – almost childlike and unsophisticated – mood. What you need are the darkened or brightened tones mentioned here for a sensuous palette and a loud, clear message that shouts: Try to resist me!

Knitwear

a flattering palette

Never one to shy away from vibrant hues, Italian fashion house Missoni celebrates colour in all its glory. Liz Griffiths, head of Creative Textile and Design Research, shares her insights on the company's iconic knitwear.

Photography **Peter Stigter**

Colour blocking, prints and high-tech structural-nylon inserts define Missoni SS 2011, a collection that boasts a palette of pop-acid yellow, orange, green and blue.

Jutting voluminous shapes sway and flutter in space. Enhancing the 3D effect are light and shadow, transparency, textured motifs, pleats and borders.

'We choose colours for their beauty and for how they interact with other colours'

What role does colour play at Missoni?
[Liz Griffiths] Colour plays an important role in our work. Twice a year we choose from 35 to 40 seasonal colours for our fabrics. We dye the thread and yarn used for these fabrics to create at least three colourways for our collections of mens- and womenswear, the latter of which includes a pre-collection and a main collection. Each season we also prepare from 12 to 15 space-dyed yarns, or *fiammatos*, which feature up to four colours.

Can you tell us more about the fiammato?
Fiammato is a space-dyed yarn – we just call it 'space-dye' – that requires a special dyeing technique: one continuous skein of yarn contains from two to four colours. This produces a random mix of colours in a single piece of knitwear. Missoni has been using this process since the business began over 50 years ago; *fiammato* is an important Missoni trademark. Three to six space-dyes are used in the menswear collection and from nine to a dozen in the womenswear collections. Each season we select innovative combinations of colour from each space-dye and create colour-related storylines for the individual collections.

What comes first, colour or pattern?
We work first with pure colour, using a mood board to find the right 'colour mood' for the collection; pattern comes later. We work with solid colours to create our space-dyes, which are something like musical compositions – but instead of notes and instruments, we have colours interacting with colours in total harmony.

In terms of colour, do you consider the specific cultural preferences of consumers who represent a variety of markets worldwide?
We always offer our customers – in all global markets – a choice; each collection features three to four colourways. We choose colours for their beauty and for how they interact with other colours to produce new colourways. We have up to 35 colours in our colour card every season. We tend to choose colours that are beautiful and flattering to most types of skin and hair colour.

How do you coordinate colours to guarantee compatibility within a complete collection?
We make about six colour cards to distribute to the different departments: print, accessories, swimwear, embroidery, menswear and womenswear. That's a good way to coordinate colours. When Angela Missoni has made a final selection of colourways and the first swatches are available, everyone is given a sample of the colourways to use as a guide and for inspiration.

And Missoni's home collection?
The colours and colour groups that we use in our fashion collections can also influence products for the home. Fashion prints are sometimes re-dimensioned and used for our furnishing fabrics. There are obvious Missoni trademarks that appear in both the home and fashion collections, but certain colourways have to be different for the home – it all depends on where they are used.

What are some of the rewards and challenges of working with colour in fashion and interiors?
It's satisfying to develop new and exciting colour moods that differ from those of the previous season, to come up with something innovative, and to generate 'colour in motion'. The biggest reward is seeing the fashion show, the finished collection, on the catwalk. The challenges lie in the process of creating a collection, especially the initial stages in which we're looking for new colours, trying to produce unusual space-dyes and putting together exciting new colour combinations for either the winter or summer season. Working with over 20 colours and mixing them together in one design can also be very challenging.

Can you recall a particular collection or project that really pushed the use of colour, either technically or conceptually?
Every season we push the use of colour to its limits. One technique, which is used to make Ottavio Missoni's Caperdoni fabrics, involves a woven knit made from space-dyed yarns mixed with different colours. The effect can be quite extraordinary. Raschel patterns using many colours and space-dyes have a stunning embossed effect.

Can you tell us more about these two techniques?
Caperdoni is a type of knitting machine that produces all sorts of patterns, from zigzags and waves to stripes and plaids. There is no limit to how many colours you can use on this machine, and it makes both lightweight and thick, heavy fabrics. The raschel is a machine from the 1920s that we use to make zigzags, waves and stripes – also in different weights.

Have you done other experiments with knitwear?
We have worked with printed chiffon, print on knit and raschel fabrics. We've used knit with fur, knit with leather, embroidered knit, felted knit, lacy knit and elasticized knit. A wide range of experiments in different fields have led to Missoni's innovative fashion looks.

How would you sum up Missoni's approach to colour?
Missoni embraces colour; it is a lifestyle.

Safety first: the art of designing the interior of a Volvo involves coordinating up to 350 individual parts, from steering wheel to door handles, to create a calm and coherent environment.

Safe drive

Corien Pompe – who heads the department at Volvo that the automaker calls Strategic Design, Colour & Material – sheds light on the process of how colour is used in automotive design.

Photography Courtesy of Volvo Car Corporation

When a customer gets into a Volvo car and feels balanced, noticing nothing distracting or out of the ordinary, the designers can feel that they've done their job properly. 'The car shouldn't look like a Christmas tree; we have to think about safety first,' says Corien Pompe. 'You shouldn't get the feeling that there are many different parts and colours inside a car; instead, you should experience a calm environment. You don't want to be disturbed by any colour differences unless the difference exists for a purpose – and then it should be *really* different.'

A colour for every component

To the untrained eye, the interior of a car may look like one continuous monotone or duotone surface. A closer look at the details, however, reveals a different story. For every Volvo car, there are 300 to 350 internal and 80 external parts, each of which has a colour. 'All surfaces on the inside and outside have a finish that includes texture, colour and effect based on the materials used,' Pompe continues. 'The dashboard and door panels have structure and colour and the wheel has colour, as does a headlight. Even the inside of the headlight has a function supported by the use of colour. There are also accent materials like wood, aluminium and fabric.'

The long-term nature of most car purchases largely determines how colour is implemented in automotive design. As a car is likely the biggest investment that the average person will make in a

'Many materials come together in a car, and we want them all to generate the same experience for the customer'

consumer product, the choice of colour is not taken lightly. For some, the car is a reflection of the owner's personality. For others, it's merely a mode of transportation and having the basics is more than enough. In addition to the price of the new car, the customer often considers its resale value. Unlike fashion design, where colours can be more fleeting, automotive design is about the long term – between four and 30 years.

Communicating lifestyle and emotion

Where does the story of cars and colour begin? 'The starting point is not the colour. The starting point is about where we want to go, what we want to communicate, what we need and want,' explains Pompe. 'It begins when we get a brief for the car, a description of the kind of driver we're designing for. We start with the consumers by making an in-depth investigation into who they are – their lifestyles, ages, locations, the whole picture.' And who might the Volvo customer be? 'People who have a desire for a "premium" product; who are focused on safety, durability and the environment; who are aware of their personal responsibilities; and who want to differentiate themselves from others.'

Of course, the lifestyle of a prospective customer differs according to car type. It's here that the car can be tailored to meet the needs of a specific customer. 'The V line (estate models) is the core of the Volvo brand, the C series (coupés) is about celebration, XC stands for "cross country", and the R design is bold and sporty.' Even though there's plenty of variety, the brand still maintains a clear identity. 'Volvo focuses on people and represents the intrinsic values of Scandinavian design.'

Which brings us back to colour. After the profile of each type of customer is considered, Volvo's designers make sketches of automobiles, indicating colour and materials. 'Sometimes we're looking for a very specific colour and sometimes for an effect that's needed to support the form, which, along with colour and material, determines the emotion involved. Colour is an important factor that – when integrated with finish, material treatment and overall appearance – entices the customer and supports the character of the product. It gives customers the opportunity to distinguish themselves and to express their individual personalities.' Younger customers, for instance, are often open to more expressive colour combinations, whereas classic cars call for the exploration of classic palettes. Whatever the outcome, the brand remains first and foremost a 'premium' choice, which implies a certain image that must be maintained. 'We are a brand that stands for longevity and care for the environment.'

Scandinavian palette

Without a doubt, the Volvo approach to colour is influenced by the scenic beauty of Sweden, where the company was founded. 'Nowhere else →

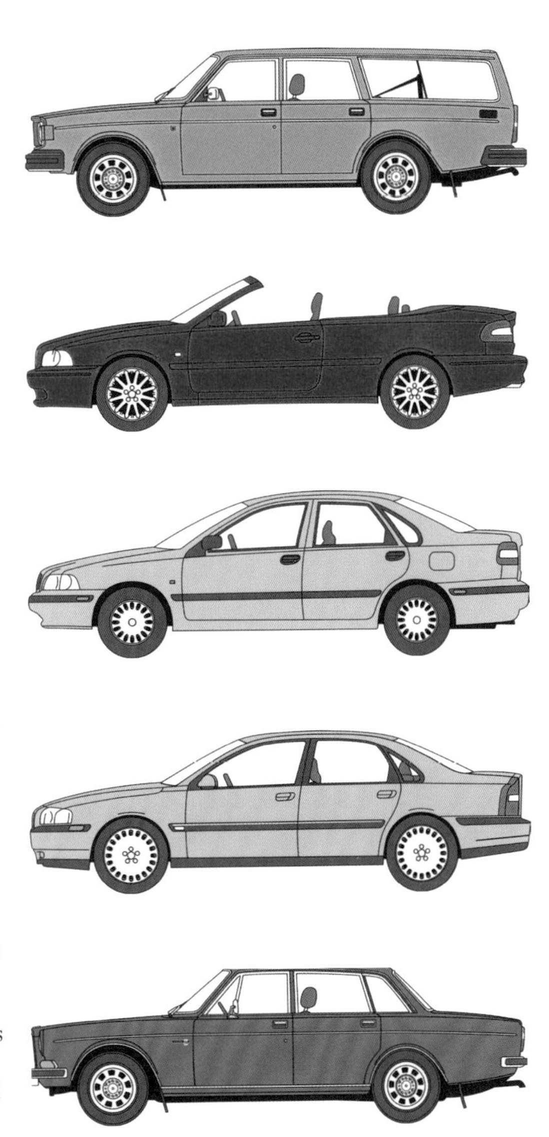

Vintage Volvo: throughout the years, the automaker's range of exterior colours has become more colourful; nevertheless, neutral shades continue to be the most popular.

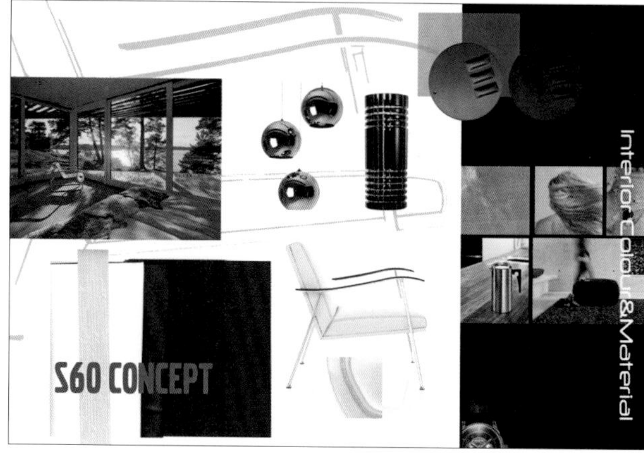

The colour and material mood boards for the S60 car.

For every Volvo car, there are 300 to 350 internal and 80 external parts, each of which needs colour

are the seasons so very different,' says Pompe, who goes on to mention 'a different look to the sunlight' in Sweden. 'Nature is our inspiration. The different seasons are marked by colours in the extreme: the colour of the sea, the needles in the black ice, the beautiful skies in autumn. We often visit the botanic gardens in Gothenburg to remind ourselves of the seasonal colours.'

She points out another factor that seems to differentiate the Volvo palette from that of rival brands. 'When Swedes think of a warm colour, they think of something with a greenish tint – a greenish beige or a grey, for example – a shade that others may perceive as cool. But the presence of yellow (in the green) creates a warmth that is very Scandinavian. Perhaps it comes from their desire for light during the long, dark days.'

Accessible personalization

After considering the profile of the consumer, the heritage of the company, and recent colour-related developments and trends, Pompe and her team select colours that will reach a wide audience while allowing room for personalization. 'The trade-in value of a car is such an important consideration at the time of purchase that the customer almost always selects a long-lasting exterior colour. The more expressive colours are important, however, and we develop them along with colours that support the timelessness of our product without compromising emotion.' Thus a palette of base colours accompanies each collection, along with dedicated colours selected for specific models.

Exterior colours

Approximately 12 base colours are selected for the exteriors of cars in each collection, and two or three dedicated colours to differentiate a particular model and lifestyle. Each model is assigned two to three solid base colours, and five to 11 metallic colours. 'For each "all new" car launch, we choose two introductory colours that best express the new product. We do this for several reasons. The colours represent the lifestyle that goes with the car, and the first cars introduced serve as models for photos and launches worldwide. The colour should be vivid and attractive for different markets, as well as the best one for showing off the highlights of the car and telling the story.' For example, an earthy green is used for the outdoorsy cross-country models and a vibrant blue for the sporty coupés.

Metallic colours and cars seem to go hand in hand. 'From all angles, metallics display a colour the best, reflecting tiny particles that highlight the form. Metallics give an extra flair, a gleam and a premium look to a car. They're trickier to produce and tougher to repair, though, which makes them more expensive.

Interior colours

Inside the car, the first step consists of defining the base colour and 'grain' of larger components, such as the dashboard and door casings. 'A grain has different tasks. Larger parts usually require a larger grain than smaller parts to "control" the surface, define the gloss level and express a certain aura.' Accent colours can be added to the car's 'furniture'.

The base colour is tested on plastic plaques before being transferred to grains and other materials; the testing phase is critical, says Pompe, because it 'defines not only the base and accent colours, but also their applications' – to plastic, to foils used on the dashboard, to carpets and so forth. Of integral importance is metamery, which has to do with the influence of different light sources on colour and of our experience of colour. 'The perception of a colour depends on its environment, which can be dark or light, surrounded by buildings or by nature. Many different materials come together in a car, and we want them all to generate the same experience for the customer. Sometimes suppliers use different pigments or materials, causing changes in reflective qualities. Getting everything aligned is a very complex and delicate process,' Pompe emphasizes. For this reason, a 'master' colour for a car's interior is selected four years before production starts, and it usually takes three years before a car with a new exterior colour is seen on the road.

Another reason for the precise standardization of base colours is longevity: they have to last at least ten years. Shared by models within a collection, base colours also continue from collection to collection, maintaining visual consistency across years of production. Along with the base colour – usually black – from two to five optional colours are among a range of interior finishes. 'We always offer customers a black interior, which accounts for 75 per cent of our sales. When people wonder why black is so dominant, I say: ask the customer! We do offer other colours, but black is always a →

Because each model is tailored to meet the specific needs and lifestyle of a specific customer, the colours on offer are intended to support the character of the car.

bestseller, although I do see a change as people become more aware of using colour and material to differentiate and personalize their cars.'

Expressive accents

Accent colours are used in car interiors as a means of expression. 'We start with a calm environment and add accent colours for impact. Accent colours allow us to refine more precisely the colours that are representative of a specific time period. Along with the exterior colour, accent colours help create the full picture of the car,' says Pompe. 'I consider materials to be colours as well. We can be more flexible by using an accent colour in the leather, thread, zippers, seatbelts or carpet.' Last but not least, because light falling through the windows affects the colour of the interior, the colour of the glass should be as neutral as possible.

Repairing colour

Colour is painted on the car not only during production; it's also used to make repairs at a later date. Since Volvo cars have a 20-year guarantee, longevity is a major consideration. Volvo has to make sure that all colours remain available for necessary repairs throughout the lifetime of the car.

Neutral vs bright

When one browses through the colours available for automobiles, the palette seems rather safe. Pompe says she's often asked 'why automobiles are so boring'. She continues: 'First of all, if the customer asks for it, we make it. We don't design for ourselves, although we do use vivid colours in some cases, because that's what entices customers into the showroom in the first place. That's what they're attracted to when they first see the car. They come in to look at a green or orange car, for instance, but leave the showroom having ordered the same car in black or silver.'

Figures for 2009 (across all brands internationally) show silver (25 per cent) and black (23 per cent) as the most popular colours, followed by white (16 per cent) and grey (13 per cent). Green, yellow and gold each account for 1 per cent. 'It's

To differentiate among the individual models and to address the lifestyles of targeted consumers, each Volvo collection is accompanied by a palette of approximately 12 base colours, along with two to three dedicated colours.

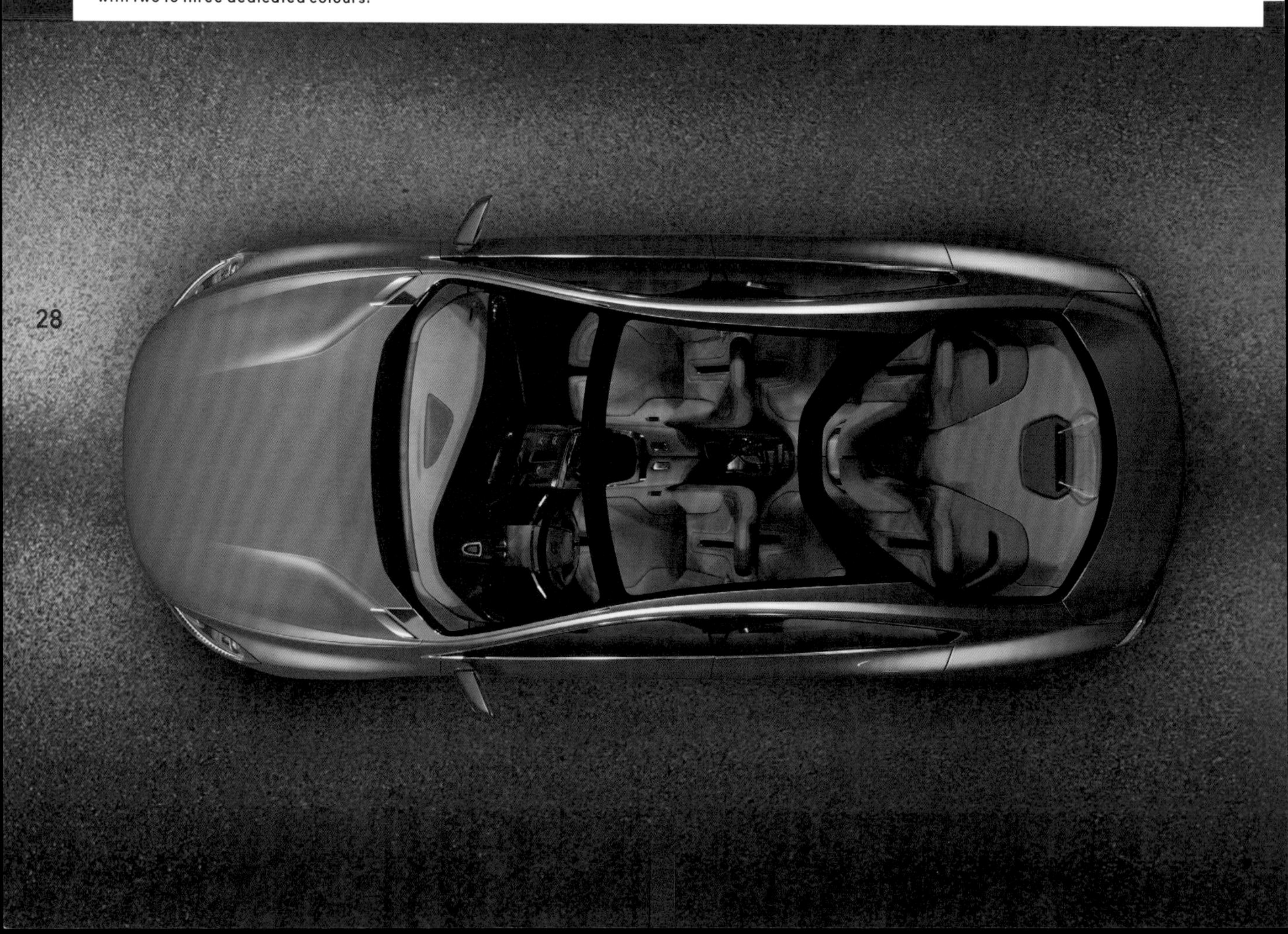

'When Swedes think of a warm colour, they think of a greenish tint — a shade that others may perceive as cool'

important to offer the customer enough choices by presenting a balanced range of neutral and vibrant colours. The basic colour is the simplest choice for people who don't want to spend more money than necessary. The more money a customer is willing to spend, the more variety they have to choose from.' Where Volvo lets its hair down a little more is in the area of 'special vehicles': limited-edition cars that allow for custom design. 'It's interesting that we see more brightly coloured Volvos in Sweden; the Swedish market seems to be more favourable to bright colours.'

Colours that sell and colours that don't

'Achromatic or neutral colours – silver, anthracite and black – are less sensitive to the year of purchase. So far, a pink car has not been a good idea, although people are more open to a variety of colours these days. We had a sporty lifestyle car in the 1980s in a forest-ranger green, a jade colour that didn't suit the car at all. It was an unexpected success and sold ridiculously well! People obviously wanted it, or perhaps we just had a good marketing strategy. We cannot foresee everything, even though with our experience it isn't just trial and error either. But surprises do occur sometimes.'

Since Volvo is a global brand, the impact of colour across all areas of the international market is also important. 'We can adjust colours to make them more appealing to customers in various regional markets. For instance, customers in the USA like beige, so we offer them more beige options. Climate also plays a role: consider how colour affects the interior temperature of a car in the tropics, even with the aid of air conditioning. But the dark winter days in Sweden, which call for a light interior, also influence the choice of colour.'

Evolving cars and colour

Since Volvo was founded in 1927, the use of colour has paralleled the evolution of the car's form. 'The shapes of cars these days – far more sculptural than earlier models – show off the entire spectrum of colours. And today we have a wider range of customers, too.

'More pigments are being developed all the time. I recently read about a "blacker than black" that absorbs a maximum amount of light and creates no reflection – a property that may be relevant in terms of safety.

'The current importance of lightweight materials – wherever we can reduce weight, we will – can also affect colour choices. One could say that we have evolved from calmer colours to more expressive colours, and from basic colours to premium colours,' Pompe concludes. 'To the sober, the elegant, the refined and the rational, we've added the emotional, thus acknowledging the presence of passion in our cars.'

Packaging

Shelf Shouting

Packaging is the most tangible representation of a brand. The stakes are high: it's win or lose at the retail shelf, which is where colour comes in.

Author Ted Mininni
Photography Courtesy of Elizabeth Arden, Courtesy of Garnier and Courtesy of Kellogg Company

The iconic red door has been welcoming guests since 1910, the year in which Elizabeth Arden opened her first day spa. The bold entranceway remains a symbol, marking the dozens of Red Door locations operating today.

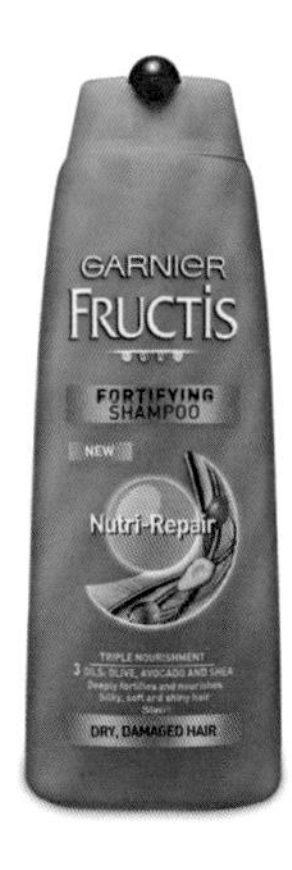

Expert design teams develop unique icons, package structure, imagery and typography, and perhaps use tactile packaging substrates along with a strongly placed brand mark to create 'ownable', one-of-a-kind packaging within a product category.

Stand in an aisle of a store. What persuades you to gravitate to a specific branded product? What is it about the packaging that piques your interest? Its unusual structural design? Bold graphics? Contemporary lifestyle imagery? Distinctive brand identity? Chances are colour attracts you first, especially when it's identified with a specific brand. When effectively conceived and executed, packaging should always refer back to the brand, leveraging its values and extending its assets. It should be a synergistic part of the overall brand expression. Packaging isn't a stand-alone marketing tool. When consumers shop, studies show that they make choices in as little as 20 seconds and ignore up to two-thirds of category products in retail environments. These statistics explain why so many products fail in the marketplace.

Owning colour, buying brands

A colour palette, distinctive graphics or imagery can eventually become iconic in packaging if consistently maintained. Imagine seeing a soft-drink can in signature red with a white swirl, missing its brand mark: Coca Cola. Would you still recognize the product and immediately recollect the brand? Surely just about everyone the world over would. Many brands are recognized instantly because of their distinctive colours. Think about Nickelodeon's signature orange and what it represents to kids. Cadbury's identifying purple is so important to the company that it sought to trademark the colour. Hot Wheels' red-and-yellow flame speaks to generations of fans. Elizabeth Arden leveraged its signature red from its iconic Red Door Salon on Fifth Avenue.

When a brand 'owns' a strong colour, it uses that hue as a calling card in its packaging. Yet colour is only one of many elements employed in packaging. Expert design teams develop unique icons, package structure, imagery and typography, and perhaps use tactile packaging substrates along with a strongly placed brand mark to create 'ownable', one-of-a-kind packaging within a product category.

All of these elements work synergistically to tell the consumer about the unique qualities and promises behind such brands. In well-executed packaging, it is this very synergy that prompts the 'buy' response in consumers. Then, if the product meets their expectations, consumers react by becoming loyal customers who continue to seek out 'their' brand, no matter how many competing products are on the shelf.

Strong examples of brand packaging include Godiva's world-famous gold *ballotin* box, embossed with the renowned icon of Lady Godiva on her horse. The packaging looks and feels luxurious, because luxury is what the brand represents. Apple's iconic logo appears on game-changing products deliberately packaged in a high-tech, minimalist black. Plain but provocative, Apple's packaging creates great anticipation in consumers who look forward to unfolding the layers within to reveal their new treasure. The legendary red 'K' on Kellogg's Special K cereal boxes has been leveraged on products in new categories, proving how effective a brand identifier can be to legions of loyal consumers. Tropicana's signature visual on its juice cartons – a straw plugged into a fresh orange – is an incredible mnemonic device. Consumers look for this icon among myriad choices packaged in orange and green. Ben & Jerry's multicoloured visuals invariably refer to the ice cream flavours, although dominating its packaging is a logo featuring the company's quintessential chunky lettering, seemingly rendered by hand within a black and yellow cartouche. This ever-hip, eco-friendly brand speaks to fans everywhere.

Thinking outside the category

Because package colour has psychological implications, companies often choose 'category' colours in a deliberate manner as a branding tool that is intended to relay information and to elicit an emotional response. In the natural- and organic-product industry, unbleached paperboard packaging rich in earth tones and touched with soft greens sends the message that this is a healthier, more sustainable brand. Luxury brands often use black, gold or silver, alone or in combination. Over-the-counter medications and supplements use blue alone, or in combination with other colours, to calm and reassure. Simpler products

When product and package come together to deliver the brand's promise, magic happens

with fewer ingredients tend to package in white.

And the result? Whole categories end up with unremarkable, hard-to-differentiate packaging. Shelves of pain-relieving brands in shades of blue, kids' toys in yellows and reds, hair care in sleek white bottles – what can a brand do to stand out?

A brand that isn't already identified with a signature colour may choose an uncharacteristic colour to distinguish itself from the expected within a product category. Even in a case where colour is a strong brand identifier, the core shade can be combined with an additional colour or colours to make a unique statement. This kind of latitude enables package-design teams to establish brand differentiation. Garnier Fructis hair care is a good example. How effective is a sinuous package structure with an unusual hinged lid in lime green when colour blocked at retail – especially when seen by consumers contemplating a sea of similar products in predominantly white packaging? When Method launched the first 8x Ultra Concentrated Laundry Detergent, it offered a uniquely structured 20-ounce package featuring a pump top. The package is easily lifted and the contents dispensed with one hand; yet this is enough detergent to clean a whopping 50 loads of laundry. Simple white packaging with blue bands, in tandem with its unorthodox structure and delivery system, makes this new detergent a show stopper.

To buy or not to buy?

The retail environment must be considered as well. Packaging cannot be developed successfully without examining the retail context, including the store layout and product placement on-shelf and within the aisle. After all, new product packaging doesn't exist in a vacuum; innumerable offerings are available in each category. To develop new packaging that will stand out from the rest, a full category analysis is a must. Mock-ups tested in sample retail settings can serve as a tool in determining whether new packaging differentiates itself favourably. Gathering feedback from consumer focus groups invited to participate in the process can help design consultants target and address potential problems during the development of the packaging, before it goes into production and is launched into the market. It takes courage to enter new territory, but, if developed and tested correctly, packaging that breaks a category's colour mould and brings a new structural element, icon or delivery system to the marketplace is likely headed for success.

Before making design and colour choices in packaging, consider these questions:

- What does the brand stand for?
- Who is the customer?
- What is it about the brand – including colour – that prompts the 'buy' response in a targeted consumer?
- When packaging products for a global audience, what cultural meanings are ascribed to the colours used? Should the palette be modified? If so, how?
- Can a unique colour – one that is unusual within the product category – be developed to support the brand? Or can the brand's signature colour be combined with another hue to achieve a distinctive look and feel?
- How does the colour or colour combination chosen for the packaging make the consumer respond during the testing phase?
- If the retailer displays fewer items from the product line on-shelf, will it colour block successfully when surrounded by myriad choices within the shelf set?

Executing packaging effectively leads to a 'first moment of truth'. The consumer 'sees' the product and is motivated to buy it within a few precious seconds. Engaging with the product leads to a 'second moment of truth'. When product and package come together to deliver the brand's promise, magic happens. Consumers either affirm a brand, if they're first-time users, or reaffirm it in their minds because it meets their expectations. Ultimately, packaging has to be judged on how it affects consumer purchasing behaviour. If packaging doesn't leverage the brand successfully by selling the product and cementing loyalty, it simply isn't effective, no matter how unique or colourful it is.

Fashion

Nuances of Grey

Staying true to its 'Japanese-ness', sports brand Onitsuka Tiger built a menswear collection around a simple element fundamental to Japanese tradition: charcoal.

Photography and video stills **Courtesy of Onitsuka Tiger**

Onitsuka Tiger's 2010 autumn/winter menswear collection was an ode to charcoal and the charcoal-based ink used in Japanese calligraphy.

Remaining true to the design concept, the team at Onitsuka Tiger blended special polyester fibres with charcoal pigment to create 'Sumi (Charcoal) Fibre Fabric' for the 2010 autumn/winter collection.

In Japanese, *sumi* refers to both the black ink used for traditional calligraphy and the charcoal from which the ink is derived. It's also the name of Japanese sportswear brand Onitsuka Tiger's 2010 autumn/winter collection, which features men's clothing and footwear in tones of black, white and ash, adorned with drops of ink. Proud of its Japanese roots, the label draws inspiration from its heritage, which Onitsuka Tiger interprets with a contemporary twist. The concepts behind the brand's collections – from dynamic cityscapes and the neon lights of Kobe, the brand's home base, to autumnal forest hues and age-old natural dyeing techniques – offer Onitsuka Tiger's international audience a glimpse of the richness of Japanese culture.

For centuries, Japan has been known for the production of fine charcoal, a cultural leitmotif in the Land of the Rising Sun. Not only the prime necessity for traditional calligraphy, charcoal is used for water purification and for preparing food. It also plays a central role in the Japanese tea ceremony, a carefully orchestrated ritual that requires designated utensils and charcoal sticks of specific lengths, which are placed in the fire that heats the water for tea.

Developing a palette for the new collection involved in-depth research. Members of the Onitsuka Tiger design team delved into the art of Japanese calligraphy. To create the graphics, they opted for charcoal-based ink and calligraphy paper. As they worked, they conferred with masters of the art to guarantee authenticity. The result – over 20 items of footwear and apparel – stays close to the source of inspiration: special polyester fibres were combined with charcoal pigment to create 'Sumi (Charcoal) Fibre Fabric', which maintains the optical values of the colours selected. In true Japanese style, however, technology enhances tradition: the *sumi* fabric is antistatic and antibacterial and features a deodorizing agent. On the Mexico 66 model, drops of ink create the brand's iconic stripes, and a subtle pattern of drops is visible on shirts and the soles of Coolidge Plus Kicks. Like a calligrapher's seal, the Japanese character for tiger is printed on the side or heel of the shoe. 'We have always been impressed by the pureness and beauty of Japanese ink,' says Shuhei Numata, senior designer at Onitsuka Tiger. 'The combination of different shades of grey and the sensitive touch of calligraphy provided inspiration.'

In terms of both colours and silhouettes, the collection is somewhat more understated than its predecessors. But it's undeniable that subtlety and refinement are as inextricably linked to Japan as neon lights. 'Charcoal and Japanese ink are both strong icons of the Japanese aesthetic,' says Numata. 'The most important thing for Onitsuka Tiger is to have all our designs strongly connected to "Japanese-ness", in which the beauty of simplicity plays a vital part.'

‘The most important thing for Onitsuka Tiger is to have all our designs strongly connected to ‘Japanese-ness’’

The ‘Sumi’ collection celebrated a spectrum of blacks, whites and ash – adorned with ink drops – a palette that prevailed throughout Onitsuka Tiger’s latest menswear and footwear designs.

Contrary to common thought according to Anne Marie Commandeur (pictured centre), colour forecasting involves no magic or crystal balls and is unable to pinpoint a 'colour of the moment'. It's all about in-depth research, analysis and strategy.

Forecasting

feeling into the future

Trend researcher Anne Marie Commandeur, founder of Stijlinstituut Amsterdam, dispels some common myths about colour forecasting and explains how it works in the mass market.

Photography **Pietro Sutera**

'Forecasting colours is like putting together a train: new trends, like train carriages, can be added'

The process behind forecasting colour trends in fashion and, more recently, interior design remains somewhat of a mystery to most people, while being widely recognized as beneficial to business. Colour forecasting is only the tip of an iceberg that includes designers, manufacturers, buyers, brands, retailers and, most importantly, consumers. Holding this all together is Zeitgeist, 'the spirit of the times', a concept used to translate the needs and emotions of society at a particular time into stories and then into colours.

But who chooses the colours, and how is it done? Anne Marie Commandeur takes us behind the closed doors of the Trend Table, a part of the Trend Forum of Heimtextil, Frankfurt's annual international trade fair for home and contract textiles. Each year a team of leading designers from six countries – Italy, Germany, France, United Kingdom, the Netherlands and Japan – meets to examine the season's trends. A different country, in rotation, leads the session annually. Commandeur, a member of the Trend Table, gives us an insight into one of the least-understood professions in the creative industries and explains why it is essential to the consumer-goods market.

How do people react when you tell them what you do?

[Anne Marie Commandeur] Many are very sceptical. They ask things like who predicted red or purple, or what colour will be popular in sweaters in two years' time. Actually, I think the problem lies in the word 'forecast'. We do have influence, but we're also part of the audience. The word 'forecast' evokes an image of a sorceress with a crystal ball, but there is no magic involved, only inspiration and clear analytical thinking.

So why do we need colour forecasting?

Inspiration and confirmation for the customers. There is an enormous mass market of people who are reluctant to make their own decisions or hesitant to choose something they haven't seen in fashion magazines or in the homes of their neighbours. Most of our fashion choices are influenced by what other people wear. This can cause problems when you want to reach a wide audience – a mass market – and you're the only one introducing a unique palette, which might not

work outside a niche market. We say that with trend and colour forecasting it's like we're putting together a train – new trends, like train carriages, can be added. One part of the industry is absolutely not interested in what anyone else is doing. They have their own identity and their own customers, who understand that identity. They find a carriage that suits their identity and their customers, and they stay on that carriage for many seasons. Others explore every new carriage, hopping quickly on or off and changing when new carriages are added to the train.

Decisions about colour are a matter of fashion and style but also of strategy. Colour is what meets the eye first when the customer is shopping. What comes next is another issue.

Do colour forecasters determine the colours that eventually appear in the shops?

In the end, we don't determine what colours people buy. There isn't a 'higher power' that decides on the right colours. Instead, colour forecasters bring diverse palettes to the industry. Many colour decisions are then made by internal design teams and buyers who have a good feel for the commercial market and know what has sold well for specific brands in the past. There are also short-term trends that influence the fast-moving brands, where it's more about ad hoc decision-making than about →

For their annual report on upcoming trends, the international members of the Trend Table dissect cutting-edge movements in design, fashion and architecture, while also studying street trends, regional influences and current consumer behaviour.

Seemingly different trends such as Alchemist (focus on textile technology and luxurious metallics) and Illusionist (tactile trickery and morphed materials) can coexist and even complement each other in a specific time period, creating variety for the consumer.

'Colour without context is nothing'

the long-term strategies that forecasters deal with. What we do know is what colour moods come through the *Zeitgeist*, but we're not absolutely sure they will all appear in the stores. There are so many shops that we see enormous variations in timing, consumers, brands and regional differences. In general, big colour flows tend to spread throughout the market, such as when the mood swings more towards neutrals, or when black is big or grey dominates, or when a trend towards vibrant colours or patterns appears.

How far ahead are your forecasts?
We're about two years ahead when considering raw materials or semi-manufactured components. For finished products, we're approximately one year ahead. We don't work on very short-term markets.

What happens when the Trend Table meets?
At the Trend Table, each team gives a presentation in which they explain their views on colour, design and innovations. When all the material has been displayed and grouped, we examine where the similarities lie. After our internal investigations and the round-table session, we develop a selection of Heimtextil trends. This we translate into a slide show, a trend film, a trend book and the Trend Forum. We prefer to work with real materials and not just a colour system, because colour is indissolubly linked with the gloss, structure and weight of a material. Hence we have our own colour cards, always set up from the beginning in various 'real' materials. We also consider the fact that we must serve various market segments, both at the level of products and in terms of commercialism and exclusivity. It is important for us to keep a certain distance from the market to provide space for innovation. When all colours have been decided, we employ a colour system that's used to communicate and print the shades.

What information and images do you share?
We all do research in the areas of influential and innovative industrial design, interior design, architecture, textile and materials, art and fashion. We share our thoughts and research on sociocultural developments and their likely influence on the market. We also share samples of textiles and colours to get a view of progress and

opportunities related to innovative technology in fibres and finishing processes. But our work is not only about innovation; it's also about cultural heritage and crafts. Past, present and future all come to the table.

Are the proposals of the various members controversial? If so, how do you handle such differences?

Controversy certainly occurs. We have to consider personal style and vision, not to mention regional differences. We try to filter all this to come up with a story that will receive wide support. It does happen sometimes that a team comes with a very personal story that we all think is interesting and should be included.

Is there one colour card for the world?

Absolutely not. There is not one colour card for the whole world at the same time. Colours are specific depending on the identity of the brand, and they are also influenced by price range, style, attitude, age of consumers and market region. We never advise clients to go outside their identity in selecting colours. Colours need to be selected for a product's specific customers.

Certain countries have their own preferences. For instance, consumers in the United Kingdom love pastels as well as black, whereas vivid colours are more popular in the USA. It's not true, however, that each Trend Table participant shows up with colours that are totally different from anything presented by the other members. We always have an overlap; between 60 to 70 per cent of the samples are identical. Everyone feels the same societal and technological undercurrents.

How much influence do manufacturers have when it comes to colours?

Manufacturers have almost no influence on colours, but the team is very aware of the market-place and the public to which trends are presented. What also happens when inspiration is transformed into commercial material is that particular colour stories or trends become clearer than others. One reason is that we work with samples from manufacturers, and their palettes are very limited at that stage.

Can you elaborate?

During the Trend Forum, we present colour trends in the form of commercial fabric samples provided by manufacturers. Such samples do not include every shade on the company's colour card. The manufacturer chooses several colours and produces enough sample material to represent the full range of possible colours. If and when orders come in, manufacturers begin production of the full colour range. For example, they might have sample materials in black at the time of the exhibition, whereas we may think a shade of caramel would better match the upcoming trend.

How important are stories to colour forecasts?

On colour cards, we see such themes as Spirit, →

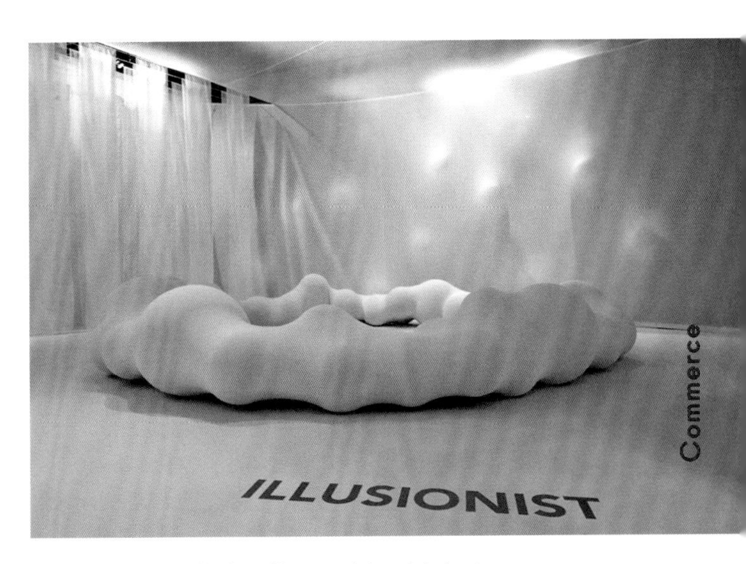

During Trend Forum the trend team envisioned six fresh trends: Illusionist, Time Traveller, Fortune Teller, Alchemist, Witchcraft, and Enchanted.

Future Traveller, De-Luxing, Whisper, Urban Jungle, Play and Mix Mash.

Colour all by itself says nothing. It says something only when it's in a context. Then you understand why, for instance, that using a lot of dark colours together reflects a dark spirit in the air. Colour without product is also nothing. Fluorescent pink can be trendy in a specific style or item, yet outdated in others.

How would you interpret a trend towards beige, for example?

A desire for beige could stem from a feeling or a need for authenticity, which translates to skins, wood, leather, nature and true woollens, such as camels and fur. In one way it's a longing for tradition and authenticity; in another it's a desire for careful, long-term investment in design and fashion. Even disregarding the economic crisis, we had seen a tendency in recent years towards authentic, natural looks – a follow-up to years of far more vivid colours. The process of colour forecasting starts with true inspiration, but it has to be linked with commercial sense, analytical thinking and an awareness of brands and audiences. The story definitely affects the colour card. Purple doesn't go well with authenticity, does it?

How has the profession changed in the past 15 years?

When I started 15 years ago, innovation was driven to a great extent by technology – a good example being fibre manufacturers. At that time they weren't very concerned about different consumer preferences; for them it was all about technology, such as being able to produce a particular shine in a fabric. But when they brought the new shiny textiles to market, the average consumer showed little interest, because 'shine' had connotations of luxury. At that time technology had too much influence on manufacturers' choices of colours and materials. Their attitude eventually led to a more market-backed approach.

Today everything moves much faster. The consumer has instant access to 'high design' in newspapers, magazines and blogs; we're seeing a democratization of design and forecasting. Everyone can be a forecaster. The hierarchy of forecasting has changed. Colour trends are no longer led solely by influential designers, artists or trendsetters; a big role is reserved for consumers as well. The street can be as inspiring as the catwalk or design event. It is important, however, to focus on trends in the larger mass-market contexts. Otherwise the industry will be incoherent – all over the map.

Do you see a relationship between forecasts in fashion and interior design?

More than ever a link exists between colours in interiors and clothes, but certain themes are still very specific to fashion. The overlap usually occurs in areas that affect both industries: will the market favour trends that are more natural or decorative or colourful or technical or soft? Interiors are

The stories around colour reveal much about the *Zeitgeist*, here seen in the visualisation of the trends Fortune Teller (free-spirited ethnic mix mash), Witchcraft (primal elements plus craft and enchanted (a fantasy world of plastic, bubble and pop).

'Coming out with identical colours for all products across the globe isn't good for business'

more pragmatic, and mood shifts are slower to occur. Yet the past decade has experienced a clear acceleration of trends and style shifts in interior and industrial design, particularly in home decoration, where style shifts are nearing the speed of fashion shifts.

Are you always right? Can you test your rate of accuracy?

We don't do quantitative research, but we do reflect on outcomes. We try to work with an eye to the future while also researching and analysing what is around today. We check to see whether something we predicted a year or two ago is currently in the marketplace. We visit fairs and shops, scour the web, look at magazines and trade journals – we're constantly informing ourselves about what's out there and what's coming. We gain more and more confidence in our process as we see our accuracy repeatedly confirmed. We realize that forecasting does influence the market, but there are always surprising, unpredictable developments. Economics, politics and social aspects can all affect the outcome of a forecast, and timing is a huge issue as well. The market is volatile and unpredictable. Although forecasted trends usually appear on the market more or less simultaneously, some brands and retailers jump directly into action, while others spread the development gradually, over longer periods. Through the years we've also recognized the growing importance of highly individualized colour stories.

Why is individualization important?

Coming out with identical colours for all products across the globe isn't good for business. What we need are variation, surprise and desirability.

Design

Colouring Consumerism

As a consultant for international brands like Apple, Swatch and Nike, Italian colour designer Beatrice Santiccioli explains why colour shouldn't be left until last.

Photography Bill Valicenti and Leslie Williamson

In the earliest stages of a project, Beatrice Santiccioli often uses collages to experiment with colours in a simple, personal way. Pictured here are the beginnings of an investigation into colour proportioning and the use of accent colours.

'Various tones of white, black, grey and silver have always been across-the-market bestsellers'

What's the first thing you do when starting a new project?

[Beatrice Santicciolі] At the beginning of a project, the client gives me a detailed brief, with information on the product in question. This brief becomes the parameters and requirements that define the direction of my colour development. During this phase of the project, I collect information and collaborate with the product designers as much as possible. Every project is unique, and that uniqueness calls for one-off solutions. My methods have to be flexible; they have to adapt to the needs of different projects. Understanding every nuance of a project influences the path I take.

Take Apple, for example. I've designed colours for the past 12 years for Apple, in collaboration with the ID Group. Our objective was to avoid following specific trends. My contribution was to design a simple yet sophisticated palette meant to enhance – and to become an essential part of – the product design. The palette is not based on specific consumer groups or sales regions; these colours have been developed through years of work and investigation and are consequently distinctive and timeless.

I also work with companies whose production cycles are based on seasons or semesters. For these clients, I investigate and forecast colours, trends and themes with an eye to creating palettes tailored to their products. Part of my research is also based on the various consumer markets, and I explore the ways in which people across the world perceive and approach colour. In the case of Swatch, the intention was to drive trends in fashion rather than to react to existing trends. Because graphics change every six months, we had to respond quickly with new colours, new graphics and new styles.

What roles do colour-related trends and forecasting play in your work?

Colour trends and colour forecasting are helpful as I gather information, ideas and moods for the coming season. What defines my work, however, are the mixtures I make with the stories, images and colours I collect during trips to Milan, the Biennale d'Arte in Venice and other places or events around the world.

How do you use these stories and images?

They suggest what I experienced at the time I saw them. The use of this information is based on the connection I see between a story or image and the project I'm working on. The final selection and editing reflect what I want to achieve and express.

Can you explain the role that stories play in developing a palette?

Stories give colours a more distinctive and comprehensive character. The story helps the colours to fit into a specific context. In projects that include multiple hues, the story works as a binder to create a coherent palette. For example, the title of a recent story, 'urban hype', featured images from street culture. The hues were vibrant, with dark and concrete-coloured accents.

How do different materials affect your work?

Materials and their specific qualities challenge the realization of a hue. During my attempt to achieve the best colour match, I sometimes have to make changes. Some colours react differently when applied to different materials, and it's not always possible to achieve the desired hue. In such instances, a great solution might be to create a new alternative – a newly developed colour – on the spot. Flexibility and open-mindedness are important to the success of a project.

Are you involved in the more technical aspects of a product, like developing new materials that allow you to apply a certain colour – or vice versa?

Yes, I have been involved in research leading to new crafts and materials, as well as in investigations into how certain products are made. A part of the work that I particularly like is the integration of colour and material. Materials sometimes have specific properties that make it difficult to create a selected hue. The process that goes into finding the best solution to the problem makes this phase of a project very interesting – and pivotal to the end result.

Often, developing a coloured material requires intense discussion about the formula: how to create the desired colour by changing a specific pigment or amount of dye, for instance. Finding a realistic way to represent colours and effects for designers and material manufacturers – before the colour has been tested in the actual material – is always a challenge.

For example, while I was designing colours for a translucent PC/ABS blend, my biggest challenge lay in maintaining the effect of light passing through the tinted plastic. Early in the project, I designed colour samples alone or with a painter, using paper, metal and an acrylic substrate. We were limited, though, without the PC/ABS that would be used in production – a material that produces a specific light effect. I resolved the problem by simply mixing dyes in vials with water, creating different degrees of translucence by adding gradual amounts of an opaque-white pigment. This was in early 1997, while I was working on iMac colours for Apple.

Could you take us through the process of selecting a palette of colours for a particular collection?

When Rick Valicenti invited me to work on the Esse project for Gilbert Paper, the challenge was to create a new, contemporary palette of colours that would last for years to come. What I did was to mix gouaches and dyes until I had an entirely new, custom-made palette. Without using any existing colour references, I came up with a total colour experience that could be perceived as a unified family of hues.

I started with a broad investigation of one-off colour samples. During a subsequent session in the lab, I worked with technicians to apply my new colours to paper pulp. Finally, I separated the paper swatches from the lab into groups and themes, from which we selected final products to be produced in different weights and textures.

What do you mean by 'a total colour experience'?

The term refers to a pure colour-creation process that tells a completely new story. Of the 16 colours in that line, only three were carried over from the previous collection. Stories accompanying the different groups were inspired by various objects and memories of mine. These memories were illustrated and explained in a book that Gilbert Paper made to launch the colour collection. Orange and bright blue were borrowed from a photograph of my mother, my brothers and me playing in a pool on the island of Ischia. Brown and pearlescent finishes referred to a kina shell I brought back from a journey to Papua New Guinea. White harked back to Ginori's classic Antico Doccia porcelain tableware.

Is it difficult to advise and develop palettes for a great diversity of clients with different aims and target groups in various cultures?

Like all design disciplines, colour design is often a game of strategy. Generally speaking, though, clients are more familiar with product design than colour design. Sometimes people need to be educated about colours and materials, and about the extra value they can add to a project when →

Paper, scissors, glue: Santiccioli's collages explore pattern, layering and colour. Underlying images are visible through the overlaid graphic.

integrated into the design process at the right time. As a consultant, I have to understand marketing and product briefs. I also go through the development process with the designer to test and define the parameters of the product.

Styles, consumer habits and colour preferences are always considered when designing a palette for a specific audience. Global markets require a more detailed investigation, which combines marketing data with information I gather from personal exploration and travel.

What were the most surprising colours that proved to be unexpectedly successful in a particular product or collection?

That's easy – the first iMac collection. For me, it's a story that really sums up how colours and design changed the way consumers looked at and felt about computers. It marked the beginning of a whole new relationship.

Can you go into more detail?

Apple took a great risk with the iMac – a brave move. The company's bold vision led to huge changes in the technology industry. The iMac represented a complete vision; colour and material were just one part of it. Before the iMac, the computer world was very homogeneous in terms of colour: warm tones, dark reds, blues, very conservative and proper. What the iMac did with its vibrant palette, translucent material and unique friendly shape was to give the user a fresh, new experience. Suddenly a functional device was also an object that was fun to use and to have at home.

Do you recall any failures? Any projects that made you think: I'll never use those colours again!

I consider it a failure to work with a client who wants a unique palette and then lacks the vision and courage to carry on, falling back into the same conventional choices. That's failure.

Has your experience led to any generaliza tions about which colours sell well and which don't?

What I've learned from the time I worked with Swatch to my collaboration with Apple is that various tones of white, black, grey and silver have

Memories, objects and stories 'borrowed' from Beatrice Santiccioli's childhood and travels – a personal journey that has also been compiled in a book – inspired a new range of colours for Gilbert Paper's Esse collection.

Emotional responses to colour guide our shopping decisions – ever wondered why the iPod comes in seven colours?

'Colour should not be added like an afterthought: make it a pivotal element of the design process'

always been – and continue to be – across-the-market bestsellers. What helps keep these colours fresh is an ongoing study of the particular hue in combination with new materials and finishes. My first project for Herman Miller, for example, was to refresh their basic palette of colours, which was made up mostly of greys and other neutral hues. My goal was to create new hues by cleaning the colours.

How do you 'clean' colours?

You basically remove the light patina that's intrinsic to the existing formula. I created a new formula for each colour by adjusting the amount of pigment or pigments. In some cases, I had to change a pigment to achieve the desired colour. The result was a crisper, more vibrant palette. Along with the addition of new finishes, the new palette was a great match for Herman Miller's product lines. Vibrant colours challenge the consumer. They're more visible, more expressive – and reveal more about the character and personality of the consumer. It takes a sense of humour, a feel for aesthetics and an extroverted personality to choose a yellow product over a more neutral model.

How much does colour influence what we buy?

I believe the consumer has an immediate emotional reaction to a hue. In the end, however, what drives most of the decisions is the combination and balance of factors, such as form, function, colour, material and cost. It depends on the product itself, but it's the totality of all those factors that ultimately motivates the customer to make the purchase. Unless, like me, she's in the habit of buying things just because they come in great colours!

Do you have advice for fellow designers? What's the most important thing to consider when working with colour?

My advice is to consider colour from the moment you begin developing the material – not at the end of your project. Colour should not be a minor detail added like an afterthought, but a pivotal element of the entire design process. Remember that you can use colour to express mood, social orientation, personal preference, tradition and ritual. Colour is a fantastic form of expression.

Wieden + Kennedy London's television commercial puts the viewer in the driver's seat, as a Honda CR-Z cruises through the city demonstrating three driving modes represented by different colours.

An rgb Experience

An RGB television commercial by Wieden + Kennedy London for Honda expresses the different driving modes offered by the Honda CR-Z.

Video stills Courtesy of Wieden + Kennedy London

The different driving modes – Sport (red), Econ (green) and Normal (blue) – highlight the changing experiences provided by the streetscape.

'The television commercial highlights how a driver's engagement with a city changes according to driving mode'

'The brief from the client,' begins Sam Heath, creative director at Wieden + Kennedy London, 'was to create excitement around the launch of something a little unexpected from Honda – the brand's new sporty coupé.' Slightly tricky to define, the car utilizes hybrid technology but incorporates the features of a sports car. What's more, it has been engineered with a three-mode driving system that enables three distinct driving experiences: Econ, Normal and Sport. 'CR-Z has been designed as the first sporty hybrid coupé to help dispel the myth that hybrids aren't fun to drive,' adds Ian Armstrong, Honda's manager of European communications.

In creating a television commercial for the Honda CR-Z, Sam Heath and Chris Groom used the RGB colour model to communicate the different driving modes. The same colours appear in the dashboard lighting that indicates each mode: Sport (red), Econ (green) and Normal (blue). Experienced from the driver's perspective, the scenes of the commercial reflect the moving car as it passes through various environments, changing driving modes, speeds and corresponding colours. The streetscapes viewed are those of Barcelona. 'Each scene was carefully created to give a clear impression of how it feels to use each mode,' says Heath. 'It was done without having to show or explain all the technicalities involved.' How was the commercial filmed? 'We used three colour filters capable of changing in intensity either during shooting or in post-production. We also shot a lot of footage without filters. This gave us the flexibility to shoot a lot of content and then, during editing, to dial the intensity or our scenes up or down.' The soundtrack consists of an ethereal monotone that speeds up with each change of mode. 'The television commercial highlights how a driver's engagement with a city changes according to driving mode. Sound and visuals work together to create a degree of suspense that makes the experience more vivid – more colourful.'

Accès NORD
ccm
ccm
ccn

Fabrics

African Pride

Luxury fashion fabric-maker Vlisco has a vivid palette shaped by a sun-kissed climate, ethnic groups and dark-skinned African beauties. Creative director Roger Gerards sheds light on the colours of West Africa.

Photography Courtesy of Vlisco

Vlisco's seasonal 'fashion collection' serves largely as a source of inspiration for consumers, many of whom have their clothing made by personal tailors.
Textile design by Henk Schellekens.

'Often consumers dislike a product with "different" hues so much that they refuse to buy it'

What role does colour play in the cultures of West Africa?

[Roger Gerards] Colours are an important ingredient used to express and to differentiate. They have a significant presence in our perception of the environment in this part of the world. The palette is quite different to that of Europe – not only the tones themselves, but also the use of colour for houses, clothing, buildings, cars, et cetera. There is an 'African' use of colour.

What makes a colour 'African'?

It's African because of its distinctive use: vivid, striking, deep colours are used on objects that are seen against the overwhelmingly natural, earthy palette of the landscape. Such contrasts are a delight for the eye. Combined with a handmade touch to everything produced here the colours are part of an honest and personal presentation of life.

Can you tell us more about the specific colours chosen by Vlisco and how you have developed them?

The development of the Vlisco palette – some 180 colours, all exclusive to Vlisco – is related to technique, history, physical environment and design. Since 1846 Vlisco has produced textiles based on the Indonesian batik technique. Along the way, starting around a century ago, products originally destined for the Indonesian market also found followers in Africa – especially West Africa and, in particular, Benin, Togo, Ghana, Nigeria, Democratic Republic of Congo and Ivory Coast.

The batik technique was transported to Helmond, the Netherlands, and then industrialized. Even today, two major steps are needed for the decoration of these fabrics: the first is a wax-resistance technique during which a drawing is 'printed' on the material by dyeing in indigo. The second involves 'blocking' the colours to the drawing. The quality of the dyes is very specific, as the desired result is a length of fabric clearly printed on both sides – each the mirror image of the other – a product characteristic of Vlisco.

With regard to our products, we recognize that some countries, regions and even individual ethnic groups have their own designs or colours. Consequently, Vlisco produces certain colourways and designs that are popular only in certain regions. Igbo women, for instance, who live in Nigeria, wear Vlisco designs in a warm yellow combined with a distinctive red. Our palette for Ghana includes bright orange, red, yellow and green. We make fabrics in green and brown for the Ivory Coast, and in yellow for Togo. In the north of Nigeria, an Islamic region, Vlisco designs need to have white areas – not blocked in colours – with no realistic objects as ornaments. However, due to increasing urbanisation, the influence of global media and the upcoming younger generation of Africans, the attitude towards the use of designs and colours that belong to certain cultural groups is changing. This gives Vlisco more freedom to create pan-African design themes and colour ways.

The colours themselves are as crucial as the regions we target and the patterns we design. Vlisco is strongly recognised by specific colour hues and the 'strength' of the colours. Even a slight difference that occurs during production can cause sales problems; often consumers dislike a product with 'different' hues so much that they refuse to buy it. This issue certainly affects those who try to copy Vlisco products: a manufacturer who doesn't have the original Vlisco dyes will make fabrics that deviate in colour from the real thing. Consumers are not fooled when they spot copies with colours that are 'incorrect'.

Consumer preference also influences the colours in Vlisco's collections. Such consumers may represent an ethnic group, but they may →

Delving deep into its rich heritage, Vlisco creates designs that add a hint of ethnic charm to the latest in city chic.
Design by Marjan de Groot.

Inspired by its lavish legacy, Vlisco rediscovers iconic designs, refines them to craft new narratives, and produces illustrative memoirs with a twist.
Design by Henk Schellekens.

also represent a country, and the two are not the same. Nigeria, for example, has around 150 ethnic groups. Merchants and traders also play a role. By ordering the same colours repeatedly, they can increase the popularity of these shades in certain areas of our market: think of the base colours of a fashion collection, which often have the same effect.

Two environmental factors also have an influence on the Vlisco colour card: the climate and the dark African skin. To begin with, the ever-present African sun fades virtually all colours; it shines 12 hours a day on every surface, including clothing. Because our original colour chart – based on Indonesian batik colours – was unsuitable, we had to develop new colours that could withstand the West African sun. The new colours required a high concentration of dyestuff; as a result, Vlisco colours are highly saturated. The bright, full, warm colours became popular for their appearance and for their quality. Consumers say that even when a Vlisco fabric is totally worn out, the colour is still intact – alive.

The second environmental factor is the skin of the black West African consumer. Even today, Vlisco consumers in Africa mention the shade of their skin in relation to the colours of Vlisco designs whose vibrant colours superbly complement the dark silhouette of their bodies. We have also been told that 'Wax Hollandais' is not for pale skin – just one more piece of evidence that the physical notion of skin has become an element of identity over the years, gaining even more importance as African nations gain their independence. A product with a certain motif in certain colours can stand for African pride.

Does the fabric itself have a symbolic meaning?

The patterns have meanings. Originally, our products featured Indonesian motifs. When the fabrics became popular in West Africa, Vlisco started to design special patterns for this market. Some include traditional African symbols or objects, but most emerge from our own ideas or relate to subjects that illustrate life in this part of the world. These motifs have *become* African.

Generally speaking, our designs stimulate 'storytelling'. The combination of motifs and bold colours make Vlisco fabrics conversation pieces: they communicate feelings, emotions, situations and so forth – often through the drawings, but also through the use of certain colour combinations. Merchants and consumers frequently name these designs, adding significance to the motifs.
A pattern's meaning often relates to the colours used, but we see this association changing somewhat as more contemporary colourways are applied to existing designs. An example is 'La Famille', which communicates family life. Many designs refer to relationships or relational problems. Power is represented by the 'sword of kinship' and education by the 'alphabet'. →

Design by Henk Schellekens.

A new and very different colour card for the West African market is highly appreciated by Vlisco's clientele.
Design by Marjan de Groot.

Design by Constance Giard.

Design by Constance Giard.

Design by Marjan de Groot.

‘The colours themselves are as crucial as the regions we target and the patterns we design’

Design by Co van den Boogaard.

Design by Marjo Penninx.

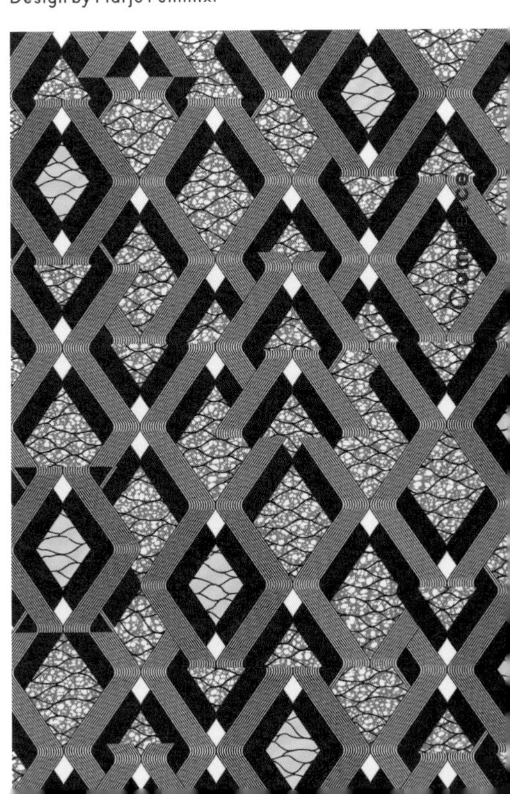

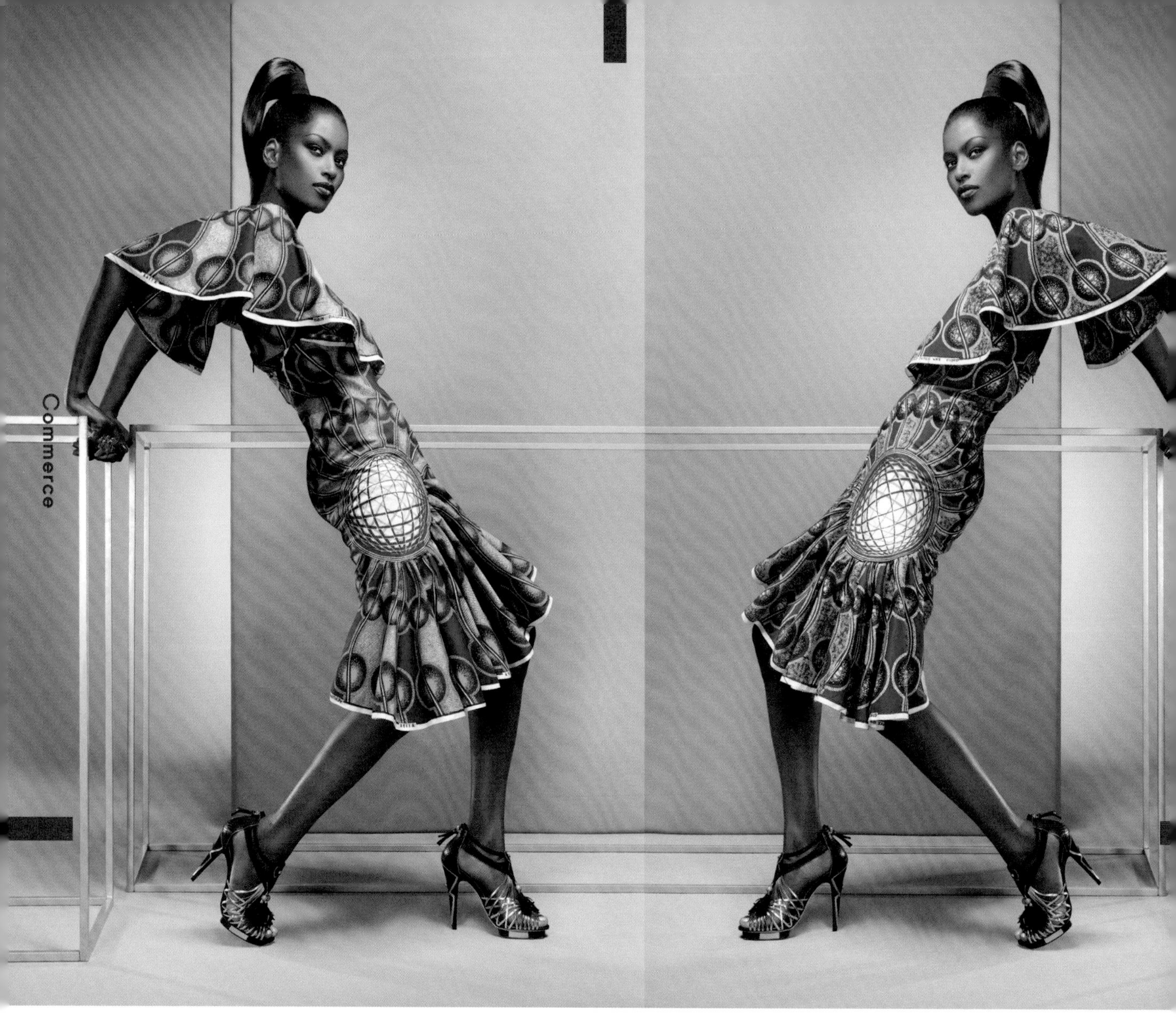

Kaleidoscopic patterns and psychedelic ornaments are the dazzling key to the Frozen Dreams collection.
Design by Nico Verbarth.

‘To withstand the ever-present African sun, our colours need a high concentration of dyestuff’

Using objects such as these makes the stories obvious. At a time when household fans were popular on the market, one of our designers, Theo Maas, incorporated a fan in the fabric he created for Vlisco. The moment of a design's launch can be the source of a story as well: a handbag print that appeared on the market just after Obama was elected was soon dubbed ‘Obama's Wife's Handbag’.

Another practice relating to symbolism is linked to important ceremonies, such as weddings. The family hosting the party may give their guests pieces of cloth in advance, in the hope that everyone will attend the event in different outfits made from the same fabric. The saying goes: ‘Behind every woman in West Africa is an overworked dressmaker’. Sharing a special occasion by wearing the same textile design is a way to add meaning to the pattern and colours involved.

What is the starting point for designs with limitations related to techniques, symbolic meanings, colours, motifs and specific consumer groups?

The Vlisco technique and the DNA of our brand design are the only limitations. Our designers have total freedom within the framework of a given collection, which takes into account a wide range of ever-changing design concepts. An important – and growing – selection of Vlisco designs is ‘replaced’ every three months with new designs in new colours. Like nearly every fashion company, we merchandise a selection of our new designs by adapting concept colours to ‘market colours’ that are popular within a particular group, region or country. Besides these more fashionable designs, Vlisco has a base collection of well-known classics that are more permanent in appearance and use; they are part of the Vlisco heritage.

In addition to following the general rules of design and working with innovative concepts, the Dutch design team finds inspiration for patterns and colours also by travelling to the Vlisco markets.

Do you take a big risk in introducing new colourways when cultural preferences are so specific?

A misconception is that Africa is static and traditional. All the women in the world, including those in West Africa, love ‘the new’. Africa is changing. Its big cities are attracting more and more people who see advantages in moving to an urban environment.

Then, too, in this part of the world there are many social occasions attended by people who pay particular attention to what they wear – even more so than in Europe. In contrast to Vlisco's more traditionally orientated consumers, Vlisco's core consumer base is made up of independent, well-educated, working West African women who attend many such occasions and who want to be fashionable. Wearing a unique, tailor-made dress in a new fabric is important to them. For this reason, we are constantly adding new designs and colourways to our more classic assortment.

We are also forced to pay attention to copies of our designs, usually made by Chinese companies who obtain the original product and have their counterfeits on the market within four weeks in most cases. Our consumers want the very newest Vlisco fabrics – the originals, not the copies.

Vlisco's philosophy is all about quality designs created from a brand-related point of view. We design new fabrics based on consistently changing concepts, motifs and colourways. And, in so doing, we link a company with a history spanning three centuries to a wide-open future. Vlisco knows that a changing world needs flexible manufacturers willing to meet the needs of changing consumers.

w h i t e

East, west, home's best

White is a mixture of all colours. It symbolizes purity, joy and innocence. The angels in early art were always draped in white. In ancient Egypt, the Pharaoh wore a white crown to verify his dominion over Upper Egypt. In India, white is the colour of holy men and women. In ancient Ireland, white represented south. To the Hopi it denotes the east, and to the Chinese the west.

White politics

White is often associated with monarchism, as opposed to other forms of government: the origins can be found in the French Revolution, when royalist rebellions attacked radical Jacobins in a siege known as the 'White Terror'. The concept re-emerged in the years following World War I, in the form of civil wars fought between the Reds and the Whites. White is also associated with peace. A white ribbon is worn by movements denouncing violence against women, and the White Rose was a nonviolent resistance group in Nazi Germany. This symbolism has deep roots that can be traced to the white dove released by Noah to test the waters. A white flag is an international sign of either surrender or truce: a signal of peaceful intent, typically in times of war.

Purer than white

In many cultures brides wear white gowns to symbolize innocence and purity. But in China and Japan, white is a mourning colour and is worn by those attending funerals. White also exemplifies cleanliness and neutrality, a logical reason for doctors to wear white coats.

White phrases

A 'white knight' is a rescuer.
'White elephant' denotes a possession too valuable to throw away and too expensive to maintain, or simply an item the owner doesn't want.
'White goods' are a description of household items such as linens, towels and appliances.

No more clutter

Like other colours, white also affects people physically. White aids mental clarity and encourages us to clear away clutter or remove obstacles. White typifies pure thoughts or actions and enables fresh beginnings.

'Never use pure white;
it doesn't exist in nature.'
Aldro T. Hibbard

Did you know that

... the ancient Greeks wore white to bed to ensure pleasant dreams?

... more shades of white are available commercially than of any other colour?

... Mount Kilimanjaro most likely derives its name from the word for 'white hill' in Swahili?

... on Yom Kippur the Grand Rabbi dresses in white to restore an amicable relationship between God and his people?

... Pantone, a global authority on colour, has reported that white is the bestselling colour of the classic American T-shirt?

... in general, white and pale flowers are more strongly scented than their darker counterparts?

'The first of all single colours is white. We shall set down white for the representative of light, without which no colour can be seen; yellow for the earth; green for water; blue for air; red for fire; and black for total darkness.'

Leonardo da Vinci

'How wonderful yellow is. It stands for the sun.'

Vincent van Gogh

y e l l o w

Yellow phrases

'Yellow journalism' refers to irresponsible and alarmist reporting. If someone is said to have a 'yellow streak', that person is considered a coward. In the United States, a 'yellow-dog contract' (now illegal) denied workers the right to join a trade union.

The significance of yellow

In most cultures, yellow is associated with the sun, the dominant force of the solar system. Yellow signifies wisdom, glory, light, joy, enthusiasm and optimism in many parts of the world. In Greek mythology, it is the colour of Mercury, messenger of the gods and conveyor of mental and spiritual enlightenment. Many Christians envision the gates of heaven aglow in golden yellow. But yellow also has negative meanings. Various cultures connect the colour to ageing and illness, as exemplified by jaundiced skin, decaying teeth and infection.

Emperors

In China, yellow is the colour of royalty. During the Ch'ing Dynasty, only the emperor could wear yellow.

Yellow fever

Put some yellow in your life when you need to make clear decisions. Yellow offers relief from burnout, panic, nervousness and exhaustion. It sharpens the memory and boosts the capacity to concentrate. Yellow is also a remedy for lethargy and depression when days are short and skies are grey.

(In)expensive dress

During the Elizabethan Era, only the wealthy could afford the yellow, colourfast dye made from saffron, which was extremely expensive. The cheap yellow dyes made from weld – used for the clothes of the poor – produced a far duller shade. Regardless of style and quality, the mere colour of a costume made it was easy to distinguish the rich from the poor.

The sporting world

The soccer referee whips out a yellow card to indicate that a player has been officially cautioned for one of a number of offences. In American football, the referee tosses a yellow flag on the field to signal a penalty. In auto racing, a yellow flag means caution, and while it's displayed cars are not permitted to pass one another. In bicycle racing, the yellow jersey is awarded to the overall leader at the end of a stage.

A safe ride

In Canada and the United States, nearly all school buses are yellow for purposes of good visibility and safety. Many taxis in that part of the world are also yellow, allowing them to be spotted from a distance.

'Yellow wakes me up in the morning. Yellow gets me on the bike every day. Yellow has taught me the true meaning of sacrifice. Yellow makes me suffer. Yellow is the reason I am here.'

Lance Armstrong

Did you know that

... in 10th-century France the doors of felons, traitors and criminals were painted yellow?

... people use yellow pan traps to capture insects, because many insects are attracted to shades of yellow?

... people who are blind to other colours can usually see yellow?

... carrying or wearing yellow gemstones is said to improve the ability to express yourself? Yellow stones also stimulate movement and mental awareness.

... even though yellow is considered an optimistic colour, people lose their tempers more often in yellow rooms and babies cry more?

... the band Coldplay achieved worldwide fame with its 2000 single 'Yellow'? The songwriters drew inspiration for the popular love song from the colour yellow.

... the message conveyed by those driving a bright-yellow vehicle is: I've got a sunny disposition and I'm young at heart? And that a yellow-gold car not only indicates money and a love of comfort, but also warmth and intelligence?

Love it, hate it

Orange, a close relative of red, sparks more controversy than any other hue. Strong positive or negative reactions to orange have been noted. Pure orange – equal parts of red and yellow – elicits a more intense 'love it or hate it' response than any other colour.

Physical orange

The colour orange stimulates activity and appetite and encourages socialization.

Oranjegekte

Orange is the national colour of the Netherlands. The royal family, the House of Orange-Nassau, derives its name in part from its former holding, the Principality of Orange (in France). Orange is the colour worn by many Dutch sports teams and their supporters. *Oranjegekte* ('orange mania') signifies the inclination of the latter to wear (often outlandish) orange outfits to sports events. In the modern Dutch flag, red replaces the original orange, but on royal birthdays a narrow orange banner hangs above the national flag.

Safety orange

Because orange and blue are complementary colours, orange objects stand out clearly against a blue sky. Certain shades – including 'safety orange' – are used to manufacture high-visibility clothing and equipment such as traffic cones, stanchions and barrels. Orange is also used by the construction industry for signs and safety jackets to warn motorists and pedestrians of pending danger and the presence of people at work.

Symbolism

Orange has different cultural meanings. In China and Japan, orange symbolizes happiness and love. The saffron stripe in the flag of India signifies courage, sacrifice and the spirit of renunciation.

r

a

n

'Orange is the happiest colour.'
Frank Sinatra

g

e

Did you know that

... the colour orange takes its name from the ripe fruit of the same name? Before this word was introduced to the English-speaking world, the colour was referred to as 'yellow-red'.

... orange or, more specifically, deep saffron is the most sacred colour of Hinduism?

... orange dye produced by using the madder root is not colourfast? And that this is why members of the lower classes often wore orange in the Elizabethan Era?

... the artist Christo and his wife, Jeanne-Claude, used 7503 saffron-coloured fabric panels for their environmental art exhibition, The Gates, which opened in New York City's Central Park in 2005?

... orange was the first scent developed for Binney & Smith's Magic Scents Crayons? After numerous reports stated that children were eating the food-scented crayons, these colours were eliminated from the selection and replaced with non-food scents.

... prisoners incarcerated in many American jails and prisons are made to wear orange jumpsuits, which make them easier to spot if they try to escape?

... 'Deluxe International orange' is the colour of the paint used for San Francisco's Golden Gate Bridge?

'California is a fine place to live - if you happen to be an orange.'

Fred Allen

'When in doubt, wear red.'

Bill Blass

r e d

Enthusiastic red

The colour red can produce all sorts of mental and physical effects. Because it's said to increase enthusiasm and stimulate energy, red is frequently used in advertising. Red may cause restlessness and insomnia if used in bedrooms, but it creates the desired dynamic atmosphere in exercise areas and playrooms.

Histor(i)ed

Ancient Egyptians called themselves the 'red race' and applied red dye for emphasis. A red flag was used by the Romans as a signal for battle. In the French Revolution, the red flag became a symbol of insurrection. When the Bolsheviks seized power in Russia, they used a red flag as their emblem, and ever since red has been considered the colour of Communism.

Passion or anger

Red is the colour of blood and, as such, clearly symbolizes life and vitality. Red zooms in on the essence of life and living and focuses on survival. Red is associated with fiery heat and warmth; it's the colour of passion and lust. On the negative side, red can signify irritability, anger or danger.

Bold, bright red

Stop signs, stoplights, brake lights and fire equipment are all bright red – a colour that's hard to miss.

It's a red world

In China, red is the colour of happiness and prosperity; it is used to attract good luck and is worn by brides. A gift of money in China is traditionally presented in a red envelope. In South Africa, however, red is the colour of mourning. Red is considered holy in some parts of Sub-Saharan Africa, and women in this part of the world are prohibited from wearing red clothes.

Physically red

When we 'see red', our anger may relate not only to the stimulus of the colour but also to the natural flush of the cheeks, a physical symptom of rage, along with increased blood pressure. Ruddy cheeks don't have to mean anger, however. A brisk run can produce the same result, not to mention love – the 'blushing bride' being a prime example.

Red phrases

To 'see red' is to be angry. A 'red herring' is a distraction, something that shifts attention away from the real issue. A 'red-eye' is an overnight aeroplane flight. If a business is 'in the red', it's losing money.

'If one says "Red" – the name of colour – and there are fifty people listening, it can be expected that there will be fifty reds in their minds. And one can be sure that all these reds will be very different.'

Josef Albers

Did you know that

... the Russian word for 'red' also means 'beautiful'?

... red gemstones are said to strengthen the body, promote will power, boost courage, increase vitality and overcome sexual dysfunctions? Carry or place red gemstones around your home or office to stimulate vitality and energy.

... at least 25 shades of red exist, from alizarin to vermilion?

... red is the colour most commonly found in national flags?

... merely perceiving the colour red can increase your metabolism by 13.4 per cent?

... Mars is called the 'Red Planet' because of the abundance of iron oxide on its surface, which produces a reddish colour?

... wearing red has been linked to increased performance in competitive activities? But controlled tests have demonstrated that wearing red does *not* increase performance or levels of testosterone during exercise. It's obviously the competitive nature of sports or games, along with the players' faith in red, that influences the successful outcome.

Chapter two

Colour & Aesthetics

GSW Headquarters, Sauerbruch Hutton's first high-rise building, put the firm's theory of polychromy into large-scale practice. The façade changes dynamically throughout the day, thanks to coloured sunshades that can be individually operated by the building's users.

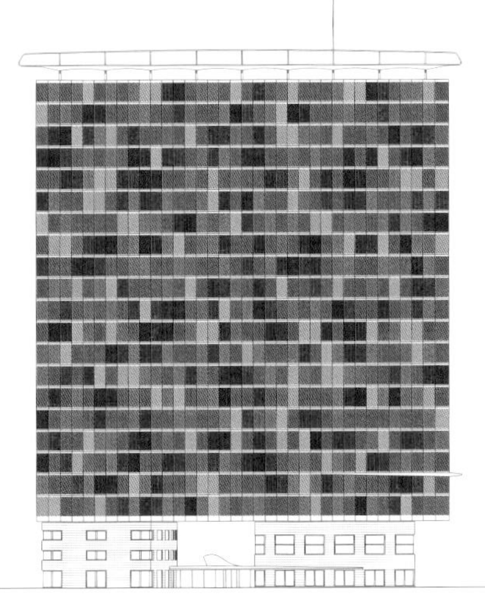

West elevation of the GSW Headquarters.

Architecture

Chromatics in Context

The use of colour by Berlin-based architecture practice Sauerbruch Hutton is rooted deeply in the relationship of a building to its immediate context. Louisa Hutton explains the firm's polychromatic tendencies.

Photography Jan Bitter, Annette Kisling, Haydar Koyupinar and Courtesy of Sauerbruch Hutton

What role does colour play in your architecture?

[Louisa Hutton] For us, colour is a design tool. Like all architects, we work with space, mass, proportion, scale and rhythm. We employ colour as an additional means to achieve particular spatial, sensual and atmospheric results. Our use of polychromy is always in the service of the main design intention and forms an integral part of our initial urban and architectural concept.

We have long been interested in perception in all its forms and in how colour can alter our visual, corporeal and haptic response to space. We approach our design work without preconceptions, and we have no pervasive dogma that governs our use of colour.

How did the fascination with colour begin?

Both Matthias [Sauerbruch] and I have long been influenced by painting. Matthias's father was a painter whose studio was adjacent to their house; my interest developed through a study of art history accompanied by visits to galleries. While these origins fostered our interest in colour, the first relatively small-scale commissions in which we were engaged from our London office were all essays in 'applied colour'. The London town houses that we worked on were typically very narrow; we found that a considered use of colour could expand the available space visually.

More recently we have found that colour can also play a prominent role in the expression of contemporary multi-layered, intelligent façades. Using colour against colour – in other words, polychromy – one can create visual space out of contrasts in tone, hue or saturation that advance or retreat in relation to one another. In this way, one can manipulate surface and depth to emphasize or counteract the bas-relief inherent in the layered façade.

What is the inspiration behind the colours in your projects?

We value the creation of buildings with personality and individuality. While the specific impulse for the use of colour varies with each project, in all cases it is founded in consideration of the relationship of the particular building to its immediate

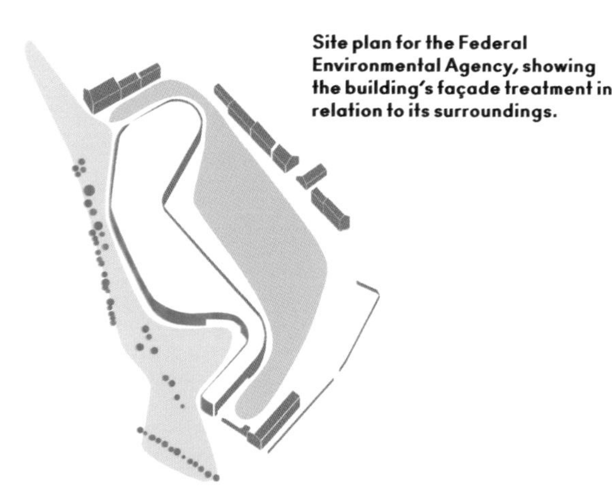

Site plan for the Federal Environmental Agency, showing the building's façade treatment in relation to its surroundings.

Composed of a mosaic of metal panels tinted in 20 colours, the pixellated façade of the Sedus Warehouse in Dogern reduces the visual mass of the building and thus its impact on the landscape.

The winding form and colour concept of the Federal Environmental Agency in Dessau prevent the building from being viewed in its entirety at a single glance. Instead, the observer sees the complex as a series of fragments.

'The building's façade is a dynamic, constantly changing painting on an urban scale'

surroundings. How conscientiously our buildings relate to their context is the measure of their quality; polychromy is one tool that we use towards this end.

For example, the colour concept of our building for the Federal Environmental Agency in Dessau supports the urban intention that this very large building is never to be seen all at once, but serially, in fragments. Firstly, the form of the building was conceived such that, through its twists and turns, its potentially monolithic expanse can never be perceived at a single glance. Secondly, variation in the chromatic treatment of the building's surface allows the diverse parts of the continuous structure to assume distinct identities with respect to their particular small-scale urban contexts. At the same time, the use of polychromy as a whole lends a specific character and atmosphere to the new location.

People often ask what our colour system is, only to be disappointed to hear that our design approach, although thorough and quasi-scientific in its iterations, is a fundamentally intuitive and nonlinear process that cannot be rationalized. We work with models of all scales; with conceptual, orthographic and perspectival drawings; and with an endless sequence of experiments, tests and mock-ups – first to clarify the concept, second to adjust the balance within the chosen colour group(s), and third to define the actual hues in combination with their specific materiality.

Which projects have been pivotal in expressing your philosophy on the use of colour, and why?

We would like to think that every project represents an evolutionary step in our work. Of course the GSW Headquarters, since it was our first high-rise project, represented an exciting challenge, as we were able to use colour on a much larger scale than ever before. Thanks to sunshades that can be operated individually by the users, the building's façade is a dynamic, constantly changing painting on an urban scale.

On the other hand, one of our main concerns in designing the Sedus Warehouse in Dogern was the integration of a large volume into a small-scale →

The selection of the two colour families in the Fire and Police Station in Berlin gives a sense of identity and legibility to the shared structure.

A floating skin of reflective coloured-glass shingles characterizes the façade of the Fire and Police Station in Berlin, providing a marked contrast between the new-build extension and the older stone and brick building.

'Greens are used for the police, while reds are employed for the fire brigade'

rural setting. The pixellated colour panels undermine the building's solidity and thereby visually reduce its impact within the landscape.

Regarding the Fire and Police Station in Berlin, our primary decision was to employ a skin of reflective glass shingles that would differentiate our addition from the solidity and absorbent matte surface of the existing neoclassical stone and brick building. The selection of the two colour families in this project gives a sense of identity and legibility to the shared structure: greens are used for the police, while reds are employed for the fire brigade.

More recently, at the Brandhorst Museum in Munich, we used polychromy to communicate a message about the content of the building as a container of art, mostly 20th-century paintings. The main theme of this message was an investigation into the independence of colour from form. Polychromy was also used in this project to break down the volume of the building within its urban context. In exploiting a play between two and three dimensions, the building's exterior design – a composition of variously glazed, vertical, ceramic sticks held off a bicoloured, horizontally folded skin – almost dematerializes the surface. The overall effect is one of multiple readings of the façade, depending on the position and movement of the viewer.

How have users, clients and the public reacted to the colour in these projects?

As in all fields of design, a bold idea will inevitably divide opinion. Strong reactions are, therefore, unavoidable. Surprisingly enough, we find that in general the public seems to respond intuitively to our spaces. Criticism tends to come from colleagues with dogmatic views on the treatment of materials.

A certain arrogance still prevails among some architects who deliberately strive to create 'timeless' architecture and who feel that fleeting trends and tastes doom any colour to obsolescence. Timeless architecture is, of course, almost never achieved, as any building is judged primarily within the sociocultural context in which it was built. We think that interesting →

The combination of two colour families not only expresses the shared use of the building – greens for the police and reds for the fire brigade – but also refers chromatically to the existing building and to surrounding trees.

'We consider colour an integral part of our architecture'

buildings – rather like interesting people – have an outspoken character that will age. Valuable buildings will have, like humans, elements to their character that will transcend their time – qualities such as elegance, generosity and poetry. However, they are first of all rooted in the context of their lifetime.

Has it been a challenge to inject vibrant colour schemes into your projects?

In architecture, colour as such is obviously an old subject that has developed into an area of permanent conflict, both in architectural circles and within the public arena. In historical examples, such as the classical temples of ancient Greece, the use of polychromy generally had an ornamental and narrative function. The application of figurative elements was intended to create an association between the building and other, extraneous themes from nature or culture. This strategy of cultural contextualization and 'sense-ualization' of a building is something that has been largely lost today. With the rise of modernism came the decline of ornamentation and thus a fundamental change in both the role and the perception of colour in architecture.

For us it is not a matter of determinedly finding a way to make our buildings colourful. As mentioned before, we consider colour an integral part of our architecture, and the particular polychromy of each of our projects develops organically from the very earliest design stages. In these beginning phases, the client is very important. Introducing the colour scheme early on helps the client to identify with the concept and to develop personal associations. For the more private spaces we design, like family homes, the client usually wants to be more involved in the colour selection than is the case with a corporate client.

What are some of the cladding materials used in conjunction with colour, and whatsort of challenges have you faced in the implementation of colour?

Printed glass has long been one of the practice's main research interests; since working on the Brandhorst Museum, we have also paid more attention to glazed ceramic. The most challenging

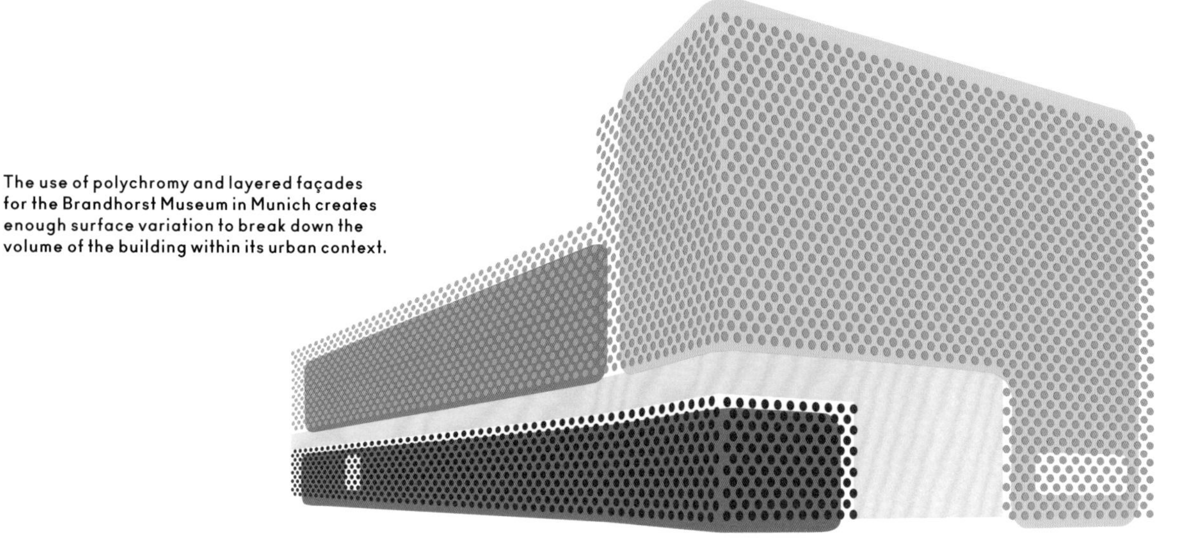

The use of polychromy and layered façades for the Brandhorst Museum in Munich creates enough surface variation to break down the volume of the building within its urban context.

The observer's perception of the Brandhorst Museum façade – with its outer layer of 36,000 vertically positioned ceramic rods glazed in families of eight colours, and its inner skin of horizontally folded metal, tinted in two colours – shifts dramatically, depending on his point of view.

part in either case is the translation of the desired colour into the actual material. This is an iterative, dynamic process of continuous exchange with the manufacturers; in the end, one is dependent upon the good eye of the particular individual who is applying the colour at the factory. In the case of the Brandhorst Museum, we visited the works at least three times during the process. In between, there were around 12 incarnations of the colour families we employed.

Do you also work with manufacturers to develop new materials or techniques that can support new colours? Do you create your own colours?

We rely on a close collaborative relationship with a few specialist manufacturers to successfully bring our ideas to fruition. We do not usually create our own colours from scratch; we use the Swedish NCS system as the main starting point for our colour concepts. In certain cases, however, we have needed to create particular new colours. In the Sheffield University project, for example, we worked back from finalized glass colours, as we needed to match these with matte paint pigments for interior walls.

Why NCS?

We were drawn to the NCS system by its unique and intuitive organization. The complex spherical colour space means we can easily see the available tonal range of any colour and compare it with others. The range of colours is reasonable – though we are experiencing an increasing need to interpolate between two or more of them – and it has been widely adopted by the manufacturers with whom we work.

What advice concerning colour would you give to other architects and designers?

The best answer I can give is to quote Kazuyo Sejima, who said, when she was asked a similar question, 'Study and practise.'

Glazes

Coming Alive

Continuing her quest to 'un-standardize' industrial production, Hella Jongerius revives the luminosity and irregularity of traditional mineral-based glazes.

Photography Gerrit Schreurs

Hella Jongerius uses traditional (natural) glazes in her search for alternatives for today's over-standardized industrial colours.

Traditional and modern colours combined on a blank canvas of 300 vases result in new hues and a richness of layering.

Jongerius researched the traditional oxide glazes used by Dutch porcelain manufacturer Royal Tichelaar Makkum, her partner in this project.

Three hundred vases, each featuring a unique colourway, are included in an experiment by Hella Jongerius, who is engaged in an ongoing investigation into the fusion of craft and industry. For her retrospective, entitled Misfit, at the Boijmans Van Beuningen Museum in Rotterdam, the Netherlands, Jongerius used white ceramic vases as a blank canvas to test the combination of traditional mineral-based glazes with today's chemical-based glazes.

Coloured Vases is the third in a series that originated with Red White (1995), which consisted of vases for which the designer used automotive spray paint rather than the bright-red ceramic paint whose cadmium content prohibited its use at that time. To continue her study of industrial colour and craft, Jongerius used standard RAL colours and the NCS colour model in her first and second series, collections that comprise 40 and 42 vases, respectively. The decision to use natural glazes for Series 3 stemmed from a desire to find alternatives for modern colours, which she believes have been over-standardized by industry owing to the need for stability and consistency.

In cooperation with Dutch porcelain manufacturer Royal Tichelaar Makkum, Jongerius researched traditional glazes, drawing from the company's centuries-old heritage. These natural oxide glazes are characterized by luminosity in colour and irregularity in concentration, which renders them unsuitable for industrial use. Currently, Royal Tichelaar uses them for a limited number of products, such as roof tiles, but no longer for porcelain.

Eventually, 150 colours were chosen from eight pigment groups. These include cadmium (red), cobalt (blue), copper (green), iron (brown), manganese (purple) and selenium (yellow). Jongerius applied these natural hues in combination with a range of synthetic glazes, which she refers to as the 'fast food' colours of today's ceramics industry, to the white vases. Each vase begins with a base of traditional oxide glaze onto which two patches of coloured transfers are added – one synthetic and one oxide. The transfers comprise a pattern of fine dots, much like pixels, that overlays the glazes and produces new hues. The final step entailed the use of acrylic paint to give 150 of the vases a little something extra. During glazing, the industrial glaze remained on the surface of the vase and the traditional glaze merged with– became part of – the vessel. The colours react to the surface of the vases to alter the observer's perception of the objects on display at the museum.

The interaction between traditional and contemporary glazes recalls the layered richness of colour found in paintings of bygone days. Polychrome hues seem to make the product come alive, as they subtly change when viewed from various angles.

The interaction between traditional and contemporary glazes recalls the layered richness of colour found in paintings of by-gone days

Installation

Sculpted Shades

Los Angeles-based architects Benjamin Ball and Gaston Nogues generate immersive installations that combine digital computation, machinery and handcraft.

Author Samantha Spurr
Photography Ball Nogues Studio, Benny Chan, Michelle Litvin and Hadley Fruits - Courtesy of the Indianapolis Museum

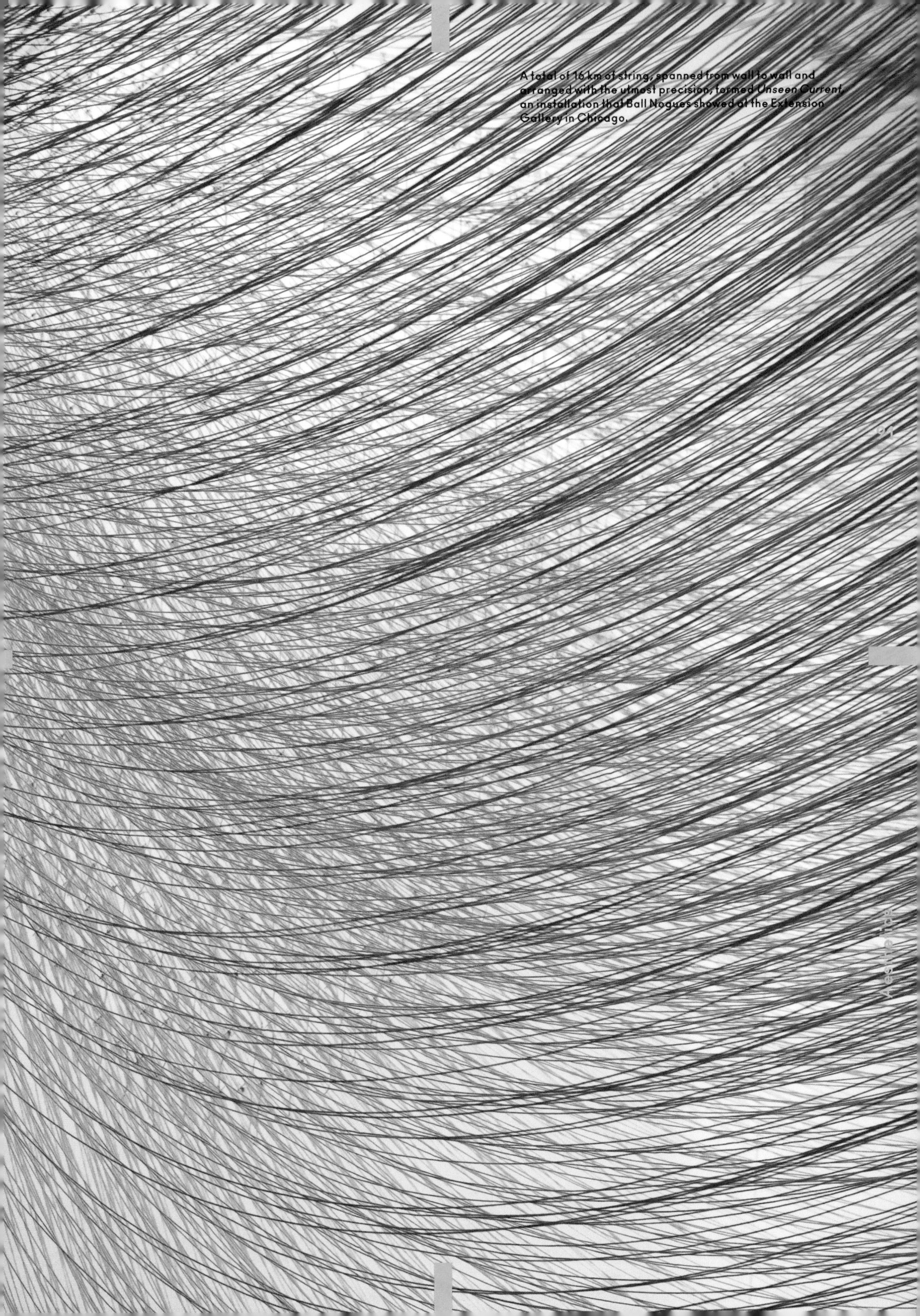

A total of 16 km of string, spanned from wall to wall and arranged with the utmost precision, formed *Unseen Current*, an installation that Ball Nogues showed at the Extension Gallery in Chicago.

The installation features a gradation from rich orange to cerulean, even though the artists used only two colours of string.

Ball Nogues has mastered the dematerialization of colour. In *Suspensions,* a series of site-specific installations, colour is something to be seen as well as experienced. Here colour takes on a spatial quality: immersive and sculptural. While there is a relationship to digital architecture in the fluid forms and undulating surfaces of these installations, they owe more to the masters of light and atmosphere: artists James Turrell and Olafur Eliasson. In *Unseen Current* (2008), *Feathered Edge* (2009) and *Gravity's Loom* (2010), thousands of strands of twine are suspended from the ceiling, creating shifting gradients of colour and form. Rather than emphasizing difference, these projects express the transformation of one colour to the next. Both utilizing catenaries, *Feathered Edge* describes the blurring of three-dimensional forms printed in CMYK, and *Unseen Current* looks to the hazy hues of the Los Angeles skies as it subtly slides from sky blue to an intense orange. The spiralling, vibrantly multihued patterns of *Gravity's Loom* delve into baroque embellishment.

The construction of the indistinct is no easy task. Benjamin Ball and Gaston Nogues are dedicated to exploring the relationship of fabrication and craft, which they find more exciting than the current preoccupation with technology and fabrication. Each project is not only about designing the object or installation, but also about designing the production. This is craft for the 21st century, a combination of labour-intensive skill and computerized fabrication technologies. For *Feathered Edge,* they used nearly 34 km of string, which is threaded and pulled through a maze of machinery as robotic airbrushes pump colour at intervals. Although the vision is more steampunk than digital, the process is configured completely by computers. Customized parametric software calculates when and where to apply colour – and how much – to each thread, while an automated cutting apparatus defines lengths. (An earlier version required arduous manual cutting.) Hundreds of packages of rolled string are then looped and knotted by hand to a printed mesh sheet that hangs from the ceiling. The precision of a computer is demanded for this operation, not to mention the painstaking care of a human being to ensure an exquisite result.

This combination of computational exactitude with the skill of making results in a unique experience of colour that transcends form while retaining a tactile and voluptuous quality.

The software automatically generated the thousands of catenaries required, computed their lengths, and prepared labels to locate each string once cut.

Custom-developed software enabled Ball Nogues to explore the form, manage the thousands of strings, and expedite fabrication.

A team of six people assembled *Unseen Current* in just seven days.

Gravity's Loom comprised an array of vibrantly coloured hanging strings that generated the appearance of a softly spiralling gossamer surface. For six months the installation twisted, contorted and spiralled down through the atrium of the Indianapolis Museum of Art, transforming the architectural space, re-choreographing the flow of visitors and encouraging new forms of interaction with the museum.

Here colour takes on a spatial quality: immersive and sculptural

Feathered Edge explored the artists' desire to alter a space with fluid architectural forms that require a minimal use of material.

Plastics

An Endless Number of Tones

With more than one million colours at her fingertips, industrial designer Sandra Hermanns shares her insights on the labyrinth of plastics and tints at BASF's designfabrik™.

Authors Sandra Hermanns and Jeanne Tan
Photography Courtesy of BASF and Konstantin Grcic Industrial Design

Accommodating the great variety of colours necessary for working in plastics, the designfabrik™ colour library includes 1,735 shades of white and 957 shades of red.

An important rule of thumb when working with plastics and colour: every product or component made from coloured plastic – no matter which type of plastic you choose – will appear to be at least a slightly different colour when exposed to different sources of light.

'Adjusting a colour requires more than simply adding a correcting shade'

Over one million 'colour impressions' can be created by combining the 20,000 colours and 70 plastic finishes available at BASF's designfabrik™ in Ludwigshafen, Germany. Potentially, this gives manufacturers a million colour choices for new products. It is this diversity and precision that make plastics popular with designers; the challenge, however, lies in finding the appropriate combination of colour, material, finish and processing technique among this complex array of options. Where to begin?

At BASF's designfabrik™, industrial designers receive advice and assistance as they design and colour their creations using plastic, from the initial seed of an idea to the product concept, the selection of colour and material, the mould design and, finally, production.

A colour for every product

Resembling a pixellated wall of colour, a corridor in BASF's designfabrik™ is lined with 20,000 colour samples, including 957 shades of red and 1,735 shades of white. Each is a unique colour that may be chosen for, say, a vacuum cleaner, a pair of sunglasses or a surfboard somewhere in the world. The plastic colour chips are arranged as a rainbow spectrum and according to special effects, textures and possible applications. While playing with colour samples gives designers an idea of how a colour will look when paired with a certain material, here they can get an even better idea of what's to come, thanks to an extensive collection of plastic objects – chairs, bottles, electronic devices and the like – that serve as 'theatre props', so to speak, which can be picked up, touched, sat on and scrutinized.

What started in 1962 as a quality-control laboratory evolved, in response to the rising demand for colours in the 1950s and 1960s, into BASF's first plastics-and-colour laboratory. Since then, plastics have opened up new horizons for designers, enabling them to combine form and function in innovative ways, particularly in the furniture sector. Consider the cantilevered chair, beginning with Verner Panton's iconic model, first produced in 1967. Made from Luran since 1971,

Panton's design has a stable structure and a glossy surface that even in the '60s could be dyed in the decade's vivid colours. Compare it with its modern day successor, the MYTO chair by Konstantin Grcic for Plank, which has a perforated seat made of Ultradur High Speed, an easy-flowing engineering plastic used mainly in the car industry prior to the launch of MYTO in 2008.

BASF's grand array of material and colour samples continues to evolve through ongoing cooperation with designers and clients.

Innovative ideas

Designers come to the designfabrik™ with ideas for new products – such as novel packaging, electrical appliances and sports equipment – many of which have never been seen before. 'Sometimes designers show up with a drawing, a sample or a mood board. At other times, all they have is a vision. Or they are just hoping to find some inspiration,' says Sandra Hermanns, an industrial designer at designfabrik™. 'Some designers have very concrete questions about how best to colour a specific object, such as the interior of a car. They need advice not only about colours but also, in some cases, about choosing the right material, finding a component design that works with plastic, integrating function or selecting the optimal production method. Our job is to turn these notions into reality.'

The right plastic

Theoretically, depending on the type of plastic used, any shape or colour is possible. Hermanns explains that BASF has five main groups of plastics: 'engineering plastics, styrenic plastics, polyurethanes, foams, and specialties like biodegradable plastics, totalling about 25 different types of materials that can be compounded, modified or combined with additives like reinforcing glass fibres'. Each new product must be matched with a material that has the right properties for that application: flexible or rigid, transparent or opaque, soft or hard, permanently or temporarily deformable, UV-protected, weatherproof, scratch resistant, biodegradable, thermally insulating →

Visitors to the BASF designfabrik™ can view thousands of colours: an astounding palette that undergoes constant modifications.

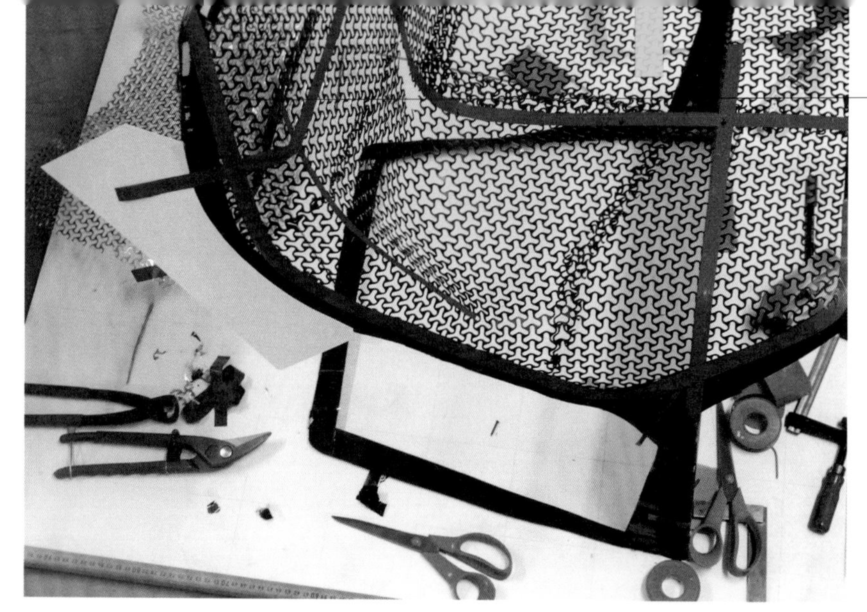

The MYTO chair designed by Konstantin Grcic for Plank is made from Ultradur High Speed, an easy-flowing engineering plastic used predominantly in the automotive industry.

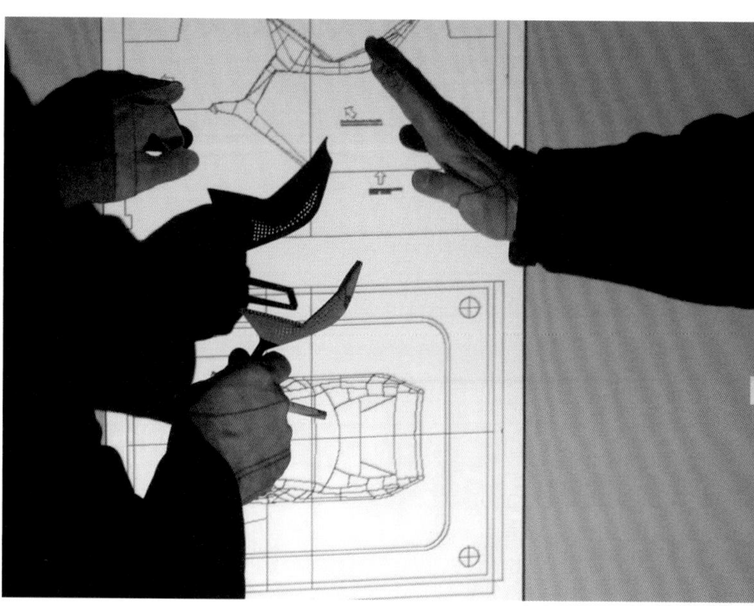

and so forth. For example, the plastic used for the MYTO chair has to be stiff and tough and have a high surface quality, even though it's been well reinforced with fibre content. The cover of a washing machine has to retain its colour (usually white) and smooth, glossy surface even after years of treatment with cleaning agents. Covers for office equipment – like printer housings – often need to be transparent in one section and translucent in another to incorporate, for instance, LED lights. For kettles, plastic parts that are in contact with metallic and heating elements have to be heat-resistant and waterproof. Mobile-phone housings should be shockproof.

A white for every white appliance

The product designer starts by choosing a material and a colour, based on the brief and the application. Then the fun begins, as an exact colour and texture are selected to match the chosen plastic. As a rule, any plastic material can be coloured. But how precise does the colour value need to be defined before the colouring process commences: in other words, how much deviation from the target value is tolerable? Exact colour matching requires a highly specific competence and cannot be achieved in all plastic materials, but it can be very closely approximated, allowing for a well-defined, precise and measurable tolerance of deviation from the target shade.

Take, for instance, BASF's 1,735 shades of white. The colour white – in all its variations – is widely used in plastics. Every brand seems to want its own version of white, especially for household appliances such as washing machines and refrigerators. White is also becoming increasingly fashionable for entertainment electronics.

Slight changes in the colour white are particularly noticeable; basically, there is no pure white. (Exposed to certain types of light, what the eye normally perceives as 'pure white' loses its immaculate look, thanks to different surface textures.) For example, the white cover of a washing machine will adopt a reddish tint when juxtaposed with a bluish-white metallic housing component on the same machine. This may result

'A colour on a glossy surface looks quite different from the same colour on a matte or rippled surface'

in an inferior-looking washing machine, since a white that does not harmonize with its surroundings invariably displays an 'impure' appearance.

How can this problem be fixed? 'Colour experts use what is known as the CIELab system, which defines a colour as a spot in a three-dimensional space,' Hermanns explains. 'Adjusting a colour requires more than simply the addition of a correcting shade; you have to take into account the exact position of the colour spot in this 3D system. In the case of a reddish-white that needs to be bluer, what you have to add – strange as it may seem – is a greenish-blue.' Thus all shades of white must be adapted with great precision to satisfy requirements relating to application, environmental conditions, light conditions (affecting the product in use) and interaction with the basic plastic material and neighbouring components. Finally, if the comprehensive selection of colours in stock does not yield the desired shade for a particular application, a custom colour can be designed on the spot.

The first off-tool chairs are tested at the BASF laboratories.

Surface and light

Colour and surface are intrinsically linked; surface characteristics play a crucial role in the effect of a given colour. At the technical laboratory of the designfabrik™, more than 70 unique surface textures can be created. This expands the number of conceivable colour impressions to more than a million. Sandra Hermann continues: 'A colour on a glossy surface looks quite different from the same colour on a matte or rippled surface. In principle, the darker the colour, the more the colour seems to change on different surface textures. During the so-called "detailed colour matching" process, varying colour impressions may result from the use of different surfaces on the same plastic, each of which refracts the light differently.'

Surface texture is determined by a mould tool. Almost every component that is manufactured by injection moulding can be created with any conceivable finish. There are limitations as to how rough the surface can be, however, owing primarily to constraints relating to the process of removing the component from the mould. Edges and round surfaces often impose restrictions on surface texture, as they can rarely be combined with very deep or broad surface structures because of the de-moulding process. Slightly differing injection-moulding conditions may also cause the colour to lose some of its shine, its brilliance. In addition, the morphology of certain plastic materials prevents them from displaying the characteristics of pigments as well as other plastics do. Thus all options and limitations must be considered, including the construction of the plastic component and the flow behaviour of the plastic melt during processing.

Light is another major factor that influences the selection of a colour. Colour exposed to different light sources (daylight, neon light, →

shopping-mall light, sunset) is perceived differently. This is called the 'metameric effect'. Such variations need not be a problem, but the possibility must be taken into consideration. If the effect produced is not what was wanted, the combination of pigments and plastics can be adjusted.

Surface and touch, curves and facets

Surface texture influences not only the appearance of a product but also its feel. The designfabrik™ has compiled a set of over 70 defined finishes that can be tested on site: leathery or smooth, technically uniform or au naturel. This is an important aspect of product development, since certain surfaces live up to the expectations created by a visual cue, while others – in the worst-case scenario – fail to do so. So-called 'phase-change materials' can even make surfaces feel cool to the touch in certain situations where, although the chosen colour does not influence the haptics of a material, it does trigger emotions that are associated with the colour. For example, you might be unpleasantly surprised on picking up a sample with a high-tech finish in a bold shiny gold to find that the object feels as soft as rubber. An orange or red object that is expected to feel warm to the touch can turn out to be the opposite when a particular plastic has been used that renders surfaces cold.

Forms with more than one surface that reflect light – each differently – are an effective way to achieve additional colour effects. Convex and concave forms, as well as edges and corners, show transitions well. And the designer can employ brilliance, reflection and/or refraction to generate a dynamic play of colour and light on the surface of an object. The same applies to transparent or translucent objects with very smooth or highly brilliant surfaces, which can produce the effect of deep colour.

Adjustments are made on a 1:1 laser-sinter model.

Dyeing plastics

Once the colour, material and finish of a product have been selected, a last, decisive step remains: dyeing the plastic.

Approximately 40 basic pigments are used at the designfabrik™. Pigments are tested under ultraviolet light and in heat and cold before being incorporated into the BASF assortment offered to designers. Because of the different melt temperatures of different plastics, the pigments must be able to withstand temperatures of up to 300°C (572°F) without undergoing any changes. Since some pigments can also influence the mechanical properties of the plastic – such as ease of flow and, in the finished product, impact resistance – the compatibility of the various colorants used in one product needs to be tested, as well as their reaction to various plastics.

Finally the pigments – from two to six – are mixed to create a specific colour formulation for each plastic. 'Precision is a must here. With transparent plastics, even one-thousandth of a per cent of pigment powder can yield a completely different colouration,' Hermanns emphasizes. The plastic-and-pigment mixture must be processed carefully. Pigments retain their true colours only within a limited temperature range and can be highly sensitive to even slight shifts in temperature. If the temperature is too high, for example, the colour may acquire a yellowish tinge.

Theory into practice

Consideration of all the aforementioned factors, each of which affects the manufacture of a design in plastic, ultimately leads to the realized product. A good example is Vegetal, a chair with a playful open structure created by Erwan and Ronan

Every brand seems to want its own version of white

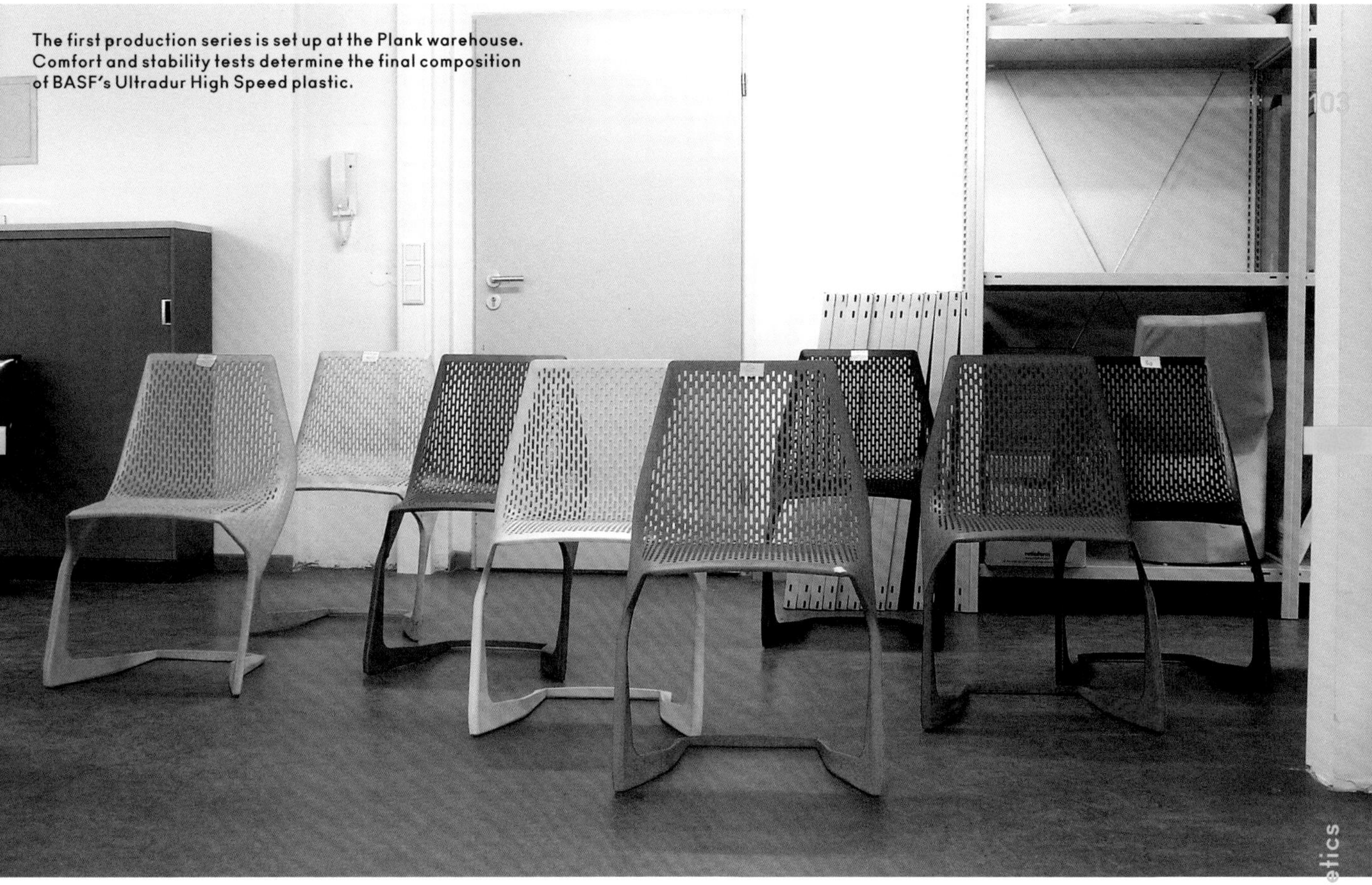

The first production series is set up at the Plank warehouse. Comfort and stability tests determine the final composition of BASF's Ultradur High Speed plastic.

Bouroullec for Vitra. With chair-shaped topiaries in mind, the brothers designed a seat intended for indoor and outdoor use. This called for a weatherproof plastic that had to be light, sturdy and easy to dye in the chosen palette of nature-inspired colours. The choice of plastic fell on UV-resistant Miramid, a material – optimized for gas injection technology (GIT) – that enables the manufacture of lightweight but stable components.

Onwards and upwards

Recent developments in BASF materials include plastics extremely resistant to high temperatures and an engineering plastic with long-fibre reinforcement able to withstand substantial loads. Each new plastic potentially reacts with pigments in a way unlike existing plastics react with the same pigments. Each new plastic must be tested and developed, therefore, to determine the best combination of material and colorant. A general rule when working with plastics is that every newly developed component made from a different material is sure to display a different colour in a different light.

BASF collaborates with designers and product developers to spur the ongoing evolution of the company's products and colours. With ample space available for new discoveries, the colour library has not exhausted all its possibilities. An endless number of hues are waiting in the wings.

Keisuke Fujiwara translates the beauty of nature's changing colours into furniture designs.

Furniture

Polychromatic Poetry

Inspired by the changing colours of nature, Japanese designer Keisuke Fujiwara uses two very different techniques to transform objects into poetic pieces of furniture.

Photography Satoshi Asakawa and Keisuke Fujiwara

An anodizing technique that causes a build-up of oxide on the surface of an object renders the colour gradation of each chair unique.

After soaking in an electrolytic bath, each piece of titanium furniture is lifted carefully from the solution. The intensity of the colour gradation is dictated by the speed of this operation.

Cover-up: two iconic Thonet No. 14 chairs were wrapped entirely by hand, using 6 km of thread in 12 'seasonal' colours.

The emotions that underlie natural gradations of colour gave rise to Fujiwara's Spool chair

Sunrise, sunset, the changing seasons: natural phenomena that clearly illustrate a gradual transformation of colours. It was the emotion underlying these gradations of colour that gave rise to Keisuke Fujiwara's Titanium series and his Spool chair.

At first glance, Fujiwara's Titanium furniture appears to be painted or dyed. In truth, the vivid colours of these pieces – belonging to a series that comprises a low table, a pedestal table and a chair quirkily titled 5 P.M. in the Summer – are the result of an anodizing technique that uses a layer of oxide to generate a coloured surface. It works like this: serving as the anode (positive electrode), the titanium piece is soaked in an electrolytic bath of water and phosphoric acid. An electric current passing through this solution releases hydrogen at the cathode (negative electrode) and oxygen at the anode, causing the build-up of oxide. The amount of voltage controls the thickness of the oxide, thus determining the colour. Vivid greens, for example, require around 110V. Colour gradations occur as the piece is lifted from the bath: the speed of this operation dictates the intensities of such gradations. The anodizing process coats the furniture in a visually striking, permanent and protective layer that is unique on each piece.

Unlike the chemical action responsible for colours in the Titanium series, the Spool chair makes use of a simple manual operation: winding thread. Here, Fujiwara sought to reinterpret the iconic Thonet No. 14 chair, showing the beauty of the handmade alongside the industrial. The designer used 6 km of thread in 12 colours for each of two bentwood Spool chairs: Fire and Water. Fire is expressed with warm hues, namely red, orange and yellow; Water is represented by cool shades of blue. Intricately wound by hand – he even wrapped the woven seats, whose surfaces resemble fine embroidery – each chair is the result of two months' work.

Glass

Pixel Perfect

The craft of glass-blowing and the colour model used by electronic systems inspired Spanish-born, London-based product designer Oscar Diaz's creation of the RGB vases.

Photography **Oscar Diaz**

Central to Oscar Diaz's vases – quite literally at the core of these objects – is a particular shade of purple that is created as light passes through a trio of glass vessels in red, green and blue.

'Colour was integrated at the beginning of the process and not applied to the surface at the end'

The exact percentage of red, green or blue required to achieve the desired shade of purple goes into each mouth-blown vase.

Diaz's overlapping colours benefit from the optical properties of glass.

Oscar Diaz's RGB vases combine the age-old craft of glass-blowing with the colour system employed by electronic equipment, such as TVs and computers. When three mouth-blown glass vases – in different shapes, sizes and colours (red, green and blue) – are nested together, the colours overlap to produce a distinctive shade of purple.

To begin with, Diaz used the computer to separate the chosen purple (Pantone 242) into its RGB components: in percentages, the colour comprises 49.3 parts red, 15.4 parts green and 35.3 parts blue. He used these precise amounts, individually, to colour three batches of glass. When light passes through the nesting trio of objects, which can be compared to a three-dimensional pixel, the colour that appears at the core of the RGB vase is purple. The form of the combined vases, each of which is about 50 cm tall, reflects the limits of this glass-blowing technique, in which molten glass is blown into large wooden moulds. Interestingly, the vases don't intentionally appear to be stackable. The striking silhouettes of the resultant vases are accentuated when combined.

'Often, objects are designed before colour is applied to them,' says Diaz. 'In this project, colour was integrated at the beginning of the process and not applied to the surface at the end. The decorative object has depth, and glass was used not only for its physical qualities but even more so for its optical properties.'

For Belgian art biennale Beaufort03, Krijn de Koning wove a garish contemporary structure through a series of abbey ruins in Koksijde to expose the hidden contradictions of the abbey's past.

tints of truth

Dutch artist Krijn de Koning challenges people's perceptions of their surroundings through vibrant architectural interventions like The Museum of Gravity.

Photography **Ernst Moritz**

A palette of intense, contrasting colours explicitly highlights De Koning's intervention, which stands out against and emphasizes the ancient brick ruins.

The ruins of the abbey are not what they seem

Overview image of *The Museum of Gravity* installation.

Archaeology met contemporary art in *The Museum of Gravity* by Krijn de Koning. The ruins of an abbey, Onze-Lieve-Vrouw Ten Duinen (Our Lady of the Dunes), in Koksijde, Belgium, provided an intriguing backdrop for the temporary site-specific installation, created for art biennale Beaufort03. Here, de Koning sought to expose the hidden contradictions of the ruins that first attracted him to the location.

The ruins of the abbey, which dates to the 12th century, are not what they seem. With little left of the original structure other than the foundations and a scattering of bricks, new layers of 'ruins' – made from different types of bricks – have been added over the years to mark what once stood on this site. 'In a way, the ruins are a fake,' says de Koning. 'The contradiction of the place is that it pretends to be a memorial to a historical reality, but that reality is problematic in its perception of historical truth.'

Through his installation, de Koning played with duality and ambiguity in an effort to expose the 'pretend reality' of the site. 'I wanted the work itself to be both integrated into and isolated from the site: integrated in the sense that it would follow the form of the ruins, isolated in the sense that it would be possible to view the work separately, as an object.' The fake ruins were framed by a rectilinear structure – 'pretend real architecture' – that wove its way through the site. Cut-out corridors and chambers that seemingly traced ruins became independent sculptural constructions that were interrupted in turn by the existing architecture. A palette of intense colours, from fuchsia to turquoise to canary yellow, highlighted the intervention, marking it explicitly as a new addition. 'I wanted the colours to provide a reality that would lend an air of excitement to the different rooms and corridors that were constructed along the fake ruins.' Contrasting colours exaggerated a shifting perspective, accentuating elements of the ruins and the surrounding landscape. 'While colour emphasized the work, making it independent of the ruins, the carrier of the colour – the form – was interwoven with the ruins. The work existed thanks to a contradiction that clearly reflected on the idea of the place as a whole.'

Fact versus fiction: the installation traces both the original and the 'fake' abbey foundations, while simultaneously creating its own surreal architecture.

For the Vegetables series, Scholten & Baijings duplicated the exact colours and structure of the fruits and vegetables used for the project in an effort to translate wonders of nature into objects made of fabric.

Design

Subtle, Sensitive, Strong

Dutch designers Stefan Scholten and Carole Baijings use colour, grids and layering to give detail to minimal forms.

Photography Merel van Beukering, Yves Krol and Takumi Ota

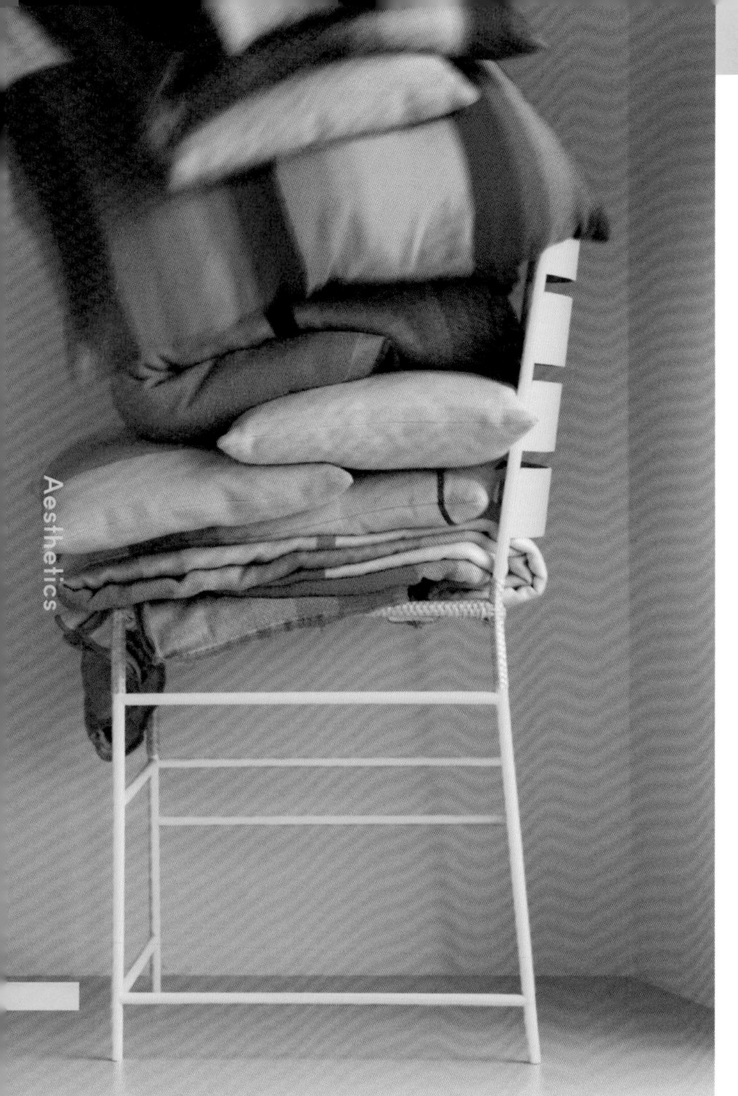

Shown here is the Pegged chair – made for Truly Dutch, a joint effort of Scholten & Baijings and the Zuiderzee Museum – in a setting with Colour Plaids and Colour Cushions.

Vivid highlights spark a subtler palette, creating an element of surprise.

An eye-catching explosion: interrupted sequences of colour enliven Scholten & Baijings' popular Colour Plaids.

Samples of table linen from Total Table Design, a Scholten & Baijings' project that emphasizes the designers' use of layering, material, detailing and colour to produce minimal forms.

A happy accident sparked the beginning of a love affair involving Dutch designers Scholten & Baijings and colour. While weaving a plaid blanket, Stefan Scholten and Carole Baijings realized that the result was not going to be as originally intended: a piece of cloth with a smooth gradation from light purple to orange. Instead of a fluid transition from one colour to another, they saw rather sharply edged stripes in an array of vivid shades. What they had created was, in fact, even more beautiful than the sought-after effect – and it gave rise to a new product. 'Ever since then, our fascination with colour has grown,' says Stefan Scholten. 'Colour has become one of our strengths. In hindsight, we recognized that mistakes can be used to our advantage – an insight that has opened up new ways of working.'

Colour and a passion for materials are signature qualities of the duo's work, which ranges from the design of furniture and textiles to tableware, using materials such as glass, wood, wool and porcelain. Theirs is a considered use of colour, in which balance is key and various hues – properly dosed to create a sense of surprise – serve as highlights. Minimal forms provide a canvas for vivid palettes, and subdued shades tone down their louder counterparts. Certain designs exhibit an interplay of colour on interior and exterior surfaces. Good examples are Table Glass, in which blinding pink is balanced with white, and Paper Table, where a few coloured accents animate a collection of simple objects. 'As the forms are quite minimal, colour alongside grids and layering gives the products an extra level of detailing,' Scholten continues. Occasionally, though, more is *more*, and a proliferation of colour, as in the designers' Colour Plaids, quite happily catches us off guard.

Rather than being a surface treatment or a last-minute afterthought, colour forms a starting point for Scholten & Baijings. 'Colour comes out of the way we design. We immediately see an object in colour,' says Carole Baijings. 'Our shapes are minimal, so we think in colour, materials and layering.' On the studio side, theirs is an investigative way of working, with many prototypes and sketches; production-wise, they combine →

The Woven Willow collection utilizes vibrant colour – in combination with the basic raw material – to inject new life into woven willow objects.

'Colour comes out of the way we design. We immediately see an object in colour'

Coloured vases are imprinted with only the 'memory' of moulds woven from strips of willow.

industrial techniques with traditional craftsmanship. The work demonstrates a sensitivity and thoroughness that can be challenging when it's time to transform designs into tangible objects. 'We're not afraid that our products or colours will be copied, because they're even difficult for us to produce!' laughs Scholten.

To learn more about their approach to colour, let's examine the methods involved and type of objects produced where each process demonstrates its own relationship to colour. Working for clients at home and abroad, these two have made everything from one-off pieces and limited editions to highly commercial products.

In Fusion

Closest to home is what the pair calls 'In Fusion', an atelier-based, small-scale operation that comprises traditional craftsmanship and industrial techniques. Colours used are geared to the techniques or materials involved. In one case, colour was used to refresh the image of woven willow wood. Dutch design publisher and distributor Thomas Eyck commissioned Scholten & Baijings to create a contemporary collection of Woven Willow objects. Crafted in the Netherlands since the 16th century, new woven-willow objects had all but disappeared from the country, with the exception of those made by a handful of hobbyists and professional weavers. Collaborating with Scholten & Baijings on this project was the only Dutch specialist making intricate wickerwork for furniture by weaving fine strips of willow into a material resembling textile. 'Our main idea was to apply colour to the willow to create a more contemporary look – to try to change wickerwork's "beige" image,' says Scholten. After choosing vibrant colours to highlight the material, they began testing ways of dyeing the willow, which is normally woven in its natural state. Success came at the end of six months of experimentation. 'Willow is a naturally oily material that repels paint. We wouldn't have been able to colour it in the past, but today's new paints made it possible,' says Baijings.

How did they do it? 'The willow needs to be made wet before weaving, and the colour needs to be well fixed before the material is ready for use,' explains Scholten. 'The fluorescent shades were particularly challenging, because they needed to go on a white base coat.' The rest is top secret. The resulting collection of eight Woven Willow objects is not an overdose of vivid colour, however. 'We respect the material in its original state, so we wanted a balance between the colours and the willow.' The Garlic Queen platter is woven *au naturel*, while the bright hues of the serviette ring are punctuated by plain willow strips. The Serious Business bowl is woven in combination with laser-cut structural plastic ribs; in one version it's the willow that's coloured and in the other it's the plastic. On a side note, the willow completely →

disappears in the Grand Bernard jug: a vessel made from coloured glass blown using a woven willow mould, which transfers only the memory of the material onto the glass. When sourcing external companies for production, Scholten stresses, it's crucial that all parties be on the same page. 'Working with colour can be difficult, because companies and craftspeople tend to use standard colours and are often not up to investigating new options. Basically, you need to work with people who also love colour.'

D:constructed

Continuing the notion of craftsmanship but moving from a small-scale to a more mass-produced operation is what the designers call 'D:constructed'. Here colour is linked to the expertise of a manufacturer, to new manufacturing technologies and to a client's specific requests. Two projects come to mind: Colour Wood for Japanese furniture-maker Karimoku New Standard; and Yellow Light, Pink Light and White Light for British design label Established & Sons.

Karimoku New Standard commissioned Scholten & Baijings to design new furniture made from *kuri* (chestnut) wood harvested from thinned forests. The company specializes in high-quality timber furniture and spray-painting on wood. Drawing from this information, Scholten & Baijings created Colour Wood: four side tables

Scholten & Baijings' Colour Wood side tables are stained to accentuate the beauty of the knots that characterize the timber; laser-printed graphics adorn the tabletops.

'Our shapes are minimal, so we think in colour, materials and layering'

Thanks to the form and carefully calculated colour gradations of Yellow Light and Pink Light, these pendants produce white light untainted by the colour of the glass.

with an interplay of texture, textile, colour and pattern. The beauty of the knots and the strong grain – sometimes seen as unwanted imperfections – are accentuated by the careful layering of a transparent coloured stain. The technique combines spray-painting overlaid with graphic grids printed by ink jet, which works on wood as well as on paper. The pair helped develop new palettes for the printer, which were rather limited at the time. Ribbons, often used in traditional Japanese design, add the finishing touch. 'We definitely challenged them to do things in a new way,' recalls Baijings.

The project for Established & Sons involved the design of a glass light fitting: the fitting was to be coloured, but the light produced was to remain white, i.e., untainted by the colour of the fitting. The solution was a pear-shaped pendant deeply coloured at the top and white at the lower edge, with a gradation so gradual it's barely visible. Instead of colouring the material itself, craftspeople carefully spray-paint the surface of the glass. 'A key to producing products in colour well,' Scholten reiterates, 'is to work with companies and craftspeople that are open to experimentation and innovation with colour.'

Delighted States

At the other end of the spectrum is Scholten & Baijings' self-initiated work: objects that don't have to be the least bit functional and colours that can be the subject of full investigation. This type of experimental work, which the designers call 'Delighted States', often ends up being purchased by museums. Take, for instance, Vegetables. 'We wanted to explore the idea of the designer as craftsman and generate a finished product made in our own atelier, where our design signature has not been translated by someone else's hands,' says Scholten of their approach to interpreting vegetables in textile. They began with abstract vegetables but soon realized they needed to go back to square one. 'We started thinking about how a vegetable actually grows. Essentially, what we did was to rebuild a piece of nature.' As their investigation continued, they identified every colour present in a particular vegetable and studied the →

The painstakingly hand-stitched rhubarb – complete with crinkled leaves, stringy texture and semi-hollow structure – features four types of fabric and 17 colours of thread.

Other stars of the Vegetables series include the artichoke and the cabbage.

transition of the colours through both structure and form. 'Once you start unpeeling nature, you see how refined the colours are,' Baijings adds. The result is incredibly detailed: cabbages, lemons, lettuce, artichokes and rhubarb that look astonishingly real and would not be out of place in the kitchen. Only their softness gives them away. A particular favourite is the rhubarb, which is composed of four types of fabric and sewed, up and down the stalk, with its perfectly reproduced semi-hollow structure, in threads of 17 colours that recreate the fibres. Gradations of pink travel up the stalk, growing lighter and ending in crinkled leaves of vibrant green and pale yellow. A seriously mouth-watering design.

Live in Colour

Lastly, through the idea of 'Live in Colour', Scholten and Baijings share their thoughts on using colour in everyday interiors, with tips for the consumer. 'Start with one thing you like in a colour that you have chosen intuitively,' says Scholten. 'You can make a grand gesture with just one product in colour.' Advice for the designer? 'To experience the challenge of working with colour, try applying the colour yourself to the material you're using.' In other words, don't be afraid to get your hands dirty. And to the design student, Baijings suggests, 'Make your own colour. Don't take it out of a jar or from a colour fan. You'll find that this is only the beginning!'

'Once you start unpeeling nature, you see how refined the colours are'

Folded-cardboard models preceded the creation of (unglazed) Paper Porcelain dinnerware, another facet of the Total Table Design collection.

Architecture

Vibrant Notes

Dutch architecture practice K2 looked to colour synaesthesia for the façades of a multi-unit residental building in Schiedam, the Netherlands.

Photography Christian Richters

Do you see what I hear? The colourful façade of Klavier, a Dutch housing complex designed by Architectenbureau-K2, is the result of synaesthesia, the phenomenon of experiencing colour in music.

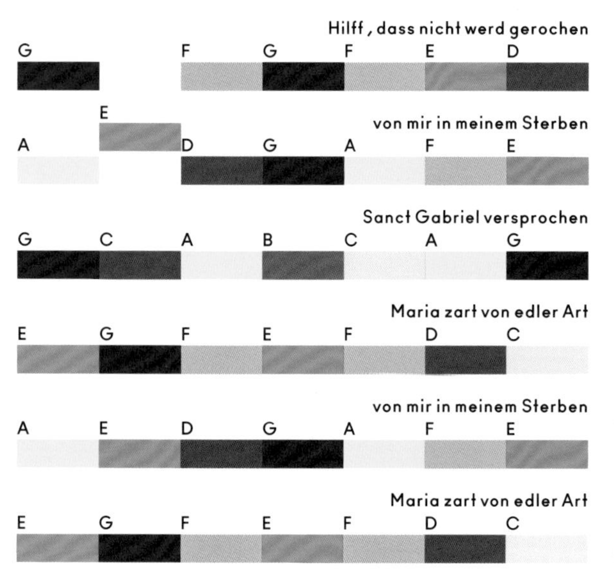

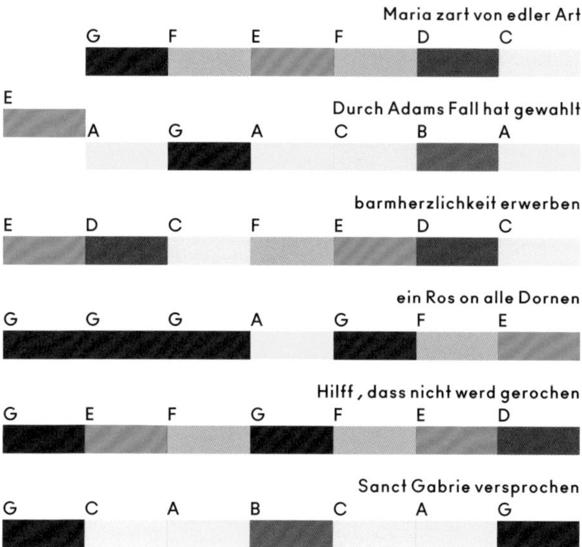

From a fragment of Jacob Obrecht's *Missa Maria Zart* that contains as many notes as the number of coloured panels needed to span the width of the façade, synaesthete Dorine Diemer selected a palette of seven colours for the housing complex.

The Klavier housing block by Architectenbureau-K2 is in a post-war neighbourhood in Schiedam, just outside Rotterdam. Until recently, this area was in desperate need of rejuvenation. The complex includes 14 mixed-use (living-working) units, each of which has two main doors that open onto public space on either side of the building. Designed to accommodate future changes, the building's load-bearing walls permit openings that allow units to be partly or wholly combined. With all this in mind, Jan-Richard Kikkert and Judith Korpershoek of Architectenbureau-K2 used a colour scheme for the façades of the various units that not only expresses the changeable nature of this housing project but also references the site.

The neighbourhood is an ode to famous composers. K2's housing block is on a street named after Jacob Obrecht, a Franco-Flemish Renaissance composer. Adopting a site-specific approach, Kikkert and Korpershoek contemplated a connection between Obrecht's music and colour, a line of thought that led to colour synaesthesia, the phenomenon of experiencing colour in music through the senses. Their search for the right colours required the help of a specialist. Dutch synaesthesia expert Cretien van Campen subsequently introduced the architects to pianist and synaesthete Dorine Diemer. Pinpointing the exact fragment of music to use was no easy task. 'Rob C. Wegman, Jacob Obrecht's biographer and a teacher of music at Princeton University, helped us to find a key work by Obrecht from 1503, the *Missa Maria Zart*,' Korpershoek recalls. 'He explained that Renaissance composers often built their compositions around a musical motif known as the *cantus firmus*. We used a fragment of the *cantus firmus* from the *Missa Maria Zart* with just as many notes as the number of coloured panels needed to span the width of the façade. The challenge lay in locating exactly the right lines of the composition to match the number of panels.'

After the music was chosen, the fragment was sent to Diemer, along with a fan deck containing thousands of Natural Colour System (NCS) samples. 'Diemer listened to the music and selected the correct colours, which we applied with meticulous care to the plywood façade panels.' Kikkert says that even though the colours do not match in any conventional way 'no one objected to the result'. Diemer proposed a rather earthy, green palette interspersed with fragments of ice blue.

Those who purchased a unit in this complex received a leaflet outlining the background of the façade colours – a clever way to keep the story alive. The legacy of the project extends beyond the walls of the housing block, however: 'To this day, when Diemer passes by and glances at our project, she's still able to sing Obrecht's *cantus firmus*.'

'We used a fragment of music with just as many notes as the number of coloured panels needed to span the width of the façade'

Diemer's colours form a harmonious yet unconventional façade, which cleverly references the neighbourhood, whose streets bear the names of renowned composers.

The dramatic explosion of blue gels that appeared in Finch's *Passing Cloud,* which he exhibited at the Corcoran Gallery's Rotunda in Washington, D.C. (2010), replicated the colour of the sky at a precise moment in time.

Art

Between Past and Present

Drawing from poetry, history and meticulous observations of the world, artist Spencer Finch creates meditative works that use colour and light to evoke memory.

Author Samantha Spurr
Photography Luke Stettner and Traeger Wolfgang

Spencer Finch's art inhabits the space between memory and experience. His installations describe a moment in time, his own or someone else's, and in the process highlight the evanescent and unique nature of experience. Finch draws his ideas from ephemeral matter – the light of suns, stars and moons; the form of raindrops and clouds. Rather than seeing the fleeting moment as eternally held in time, the American artist re-creates an event using what he sees as the one constant: light. Despite the changes wrought on places by time, it is the light – a kind of visceral time capsule that ignites one re-experience of an event – that remains the same.

Colour calibration

To work with light is to work with colour. Light is manifest in these artworks through colour. It is colour that lends light texture, that gives light its uniqueness, thereby situating light in time. Colour is used not simply as something applied to a surface, but as a spatial substance. Finch begins his projects with a measured, objective analysis of the scenario. Technology allows for careful calibration of many of these works, transposing experience into data, from which Finch extrapolates his art. On 10 March 2009, Finch used a colour meter to measure the colour spectrum of moonlight during one Venetian evening. His installation for the International Art Exhibition at the Venice Biennale that year consisted of coloured filters applied to a series of windows. Shades of blue punctuated by saffron, umber and peach shifted sunlight into moonlight. Photographs of the project too easily focus on the vibrant fenestration, but it is the spectrum of tinted light that fills and moves across the room that is the true work of art. The filters transformed the springtime light into the colours of a moonlit evening in a kind of alchemic metamorphosis that occurred each day in the exhibition space.

In that same year, Finch installed *The River That Flows Both Ways* at the High Line in New York City. The title is a translation of the Native American name for the Hudson River, a word referencing the tidal dynamics of the waterway.

Colour becomes a medium to imprint memory onto someone's conscience

Wandering along the elevated pathway of the High Line in New York City, pedestrians passed Finch's site-specific work, *The River That Flows Both Ways* (2009), subtly installed into the walls of the disused Chelsea Market Tunnel. The work of art invited passers-by to experience the changing colours of the Hudson River – which actually flows in two directions – throughout the day and through the seasons.

An overlay and patterning of colours merged in the medieval interior that Spencer Finch created for the 2009 Venice Biennale. *Moonlight* filled the space with a serenely mystical ambience.

Finch saw in the eddying waters a rich palette not usually associated with the Hudson, this stretch of which the High Line – an elevated park situated on disused rail tracks – has reconnected with the city. One day Finch sat in a tugboat on the river for nearly 12 hours while taking one photo a minute of the 'same part of the water'. Back in his studio, he examined 700 images, extracted one pixel from each image and matched it to a specific colour. The next step was to transfer the result to a printed film, which was laminated between two pieces of glass. The result was a colour chart of the Hudson River as viewed from a particular boat on a particular day. The 700 colours fill 700 panes of glass featured in a former High Line loading dock. Muted sea greys, greens and pale whites form a pattern that responds to the light of the passing day, changing on land as they did on water.

Spatial narratives

Finch says that 'to be contemporary means to be aware of history'. Uninterested in abstraction, he describes himself as 'a representational artist'. Although his projects initially appear to sit within the context of contemporary atmospheric artists such as James Turrell and Olafur Eliasson, viewers discover that a historical narrative is an integral part of engaging with Finch's work. Such a narrative moves the viewer into his art, overlaying the subjective experience with a patina of history. 'There is always a paradox inherent in vision, an impossible desire to see yourself seeing,' says Finch. 'A lot of my work probes this tension – wanting to see, but being unable to see.' Finch's ability to capture the qualitative experience of a specific moment was encapsulated in *Passing Cloud* (2010), a site-specific project made for the Corcoran Gallery's Rotunda in Washington. D.C. The impetus for this work emerged from the geographical and temporal intersection of two important figures in American history: Abraham Lincoln and Walt Whitman. The project focused on a certain junction in Washington where the two are said to have crossed paths. Instead of examining the geography, Finch looked up at the sky and posed this question: 'What is the same about →

Washington now as it was then, because the city has changed so much?' His answer? 'One thing that is the same is the light, which is almost, almost nothing.' Photographs of Finch's work are always deceptive, as they show tangible objects rather than the space around them. It is too easy to see *Passing Cloud* as a hanging mass of blue gels, an obese, pantomimic chandelier. Here again Finch has created the dynamic, spatial qualities of the site and not a static object. A clearer image lies in the smoky blues and deep purples reflected in the parquetry flooring. But Finch's ambition was to capture the light of the sky, the space between object and floor. Passing beneath the suspended structure, visitors may have noticed the light on their skin or clothes changing as they crossed the room, simulating the moment a cloud drifting by left its shadow on the Lincoln-Whitman intersection.

In *Two Examples of Molecular Orbital Theory (Prussian Blue)*, a work from 2005, the question was one of perception. Positioned side by side, two apparently identical rooms emanated the same shade of blue light. Generating the blue light in one room, however, were fluorescent bulbs with blue gel filters (blue light, white walls), while the other was the result of fluorescent bulbs without filters illuminating blue wall paint (white light, blue walls). The overall result was a spatial study in the molecular structure of the Prussian-blue pigment and the derivation of colours through very different physical and material relations.

Cinematic colour space

Finch exposes the mechanics of the artificially constructed experience. Rather than forging authenticity, he tells a story of its making, which contributes to the experience of his work. The low-tech quality of Finch's art underscores his claim that he is uninterested in illusion. He often uses materials found in his studio: lamp parts and light bulbs, fluorescent tubes, theatrical lighting gels and filters, stained glass and candles. A 2007 project, *West (Sunset in My Motel Room, Monument Valley, February 26, 2007, 5.36-6.06 PM)*, featured nine video monitors switched on but

Colour is used not simply as something applied to a surface, but as a spatial substance

A photograph of *Two Examples of Molecular Orbital Theory (Prussian Blue*, 2005) betrays the deception of a work that seems to feature two identically lit rooms. In reality, the light has been painstakingly produced using different methods to create the same atmospheric colour.

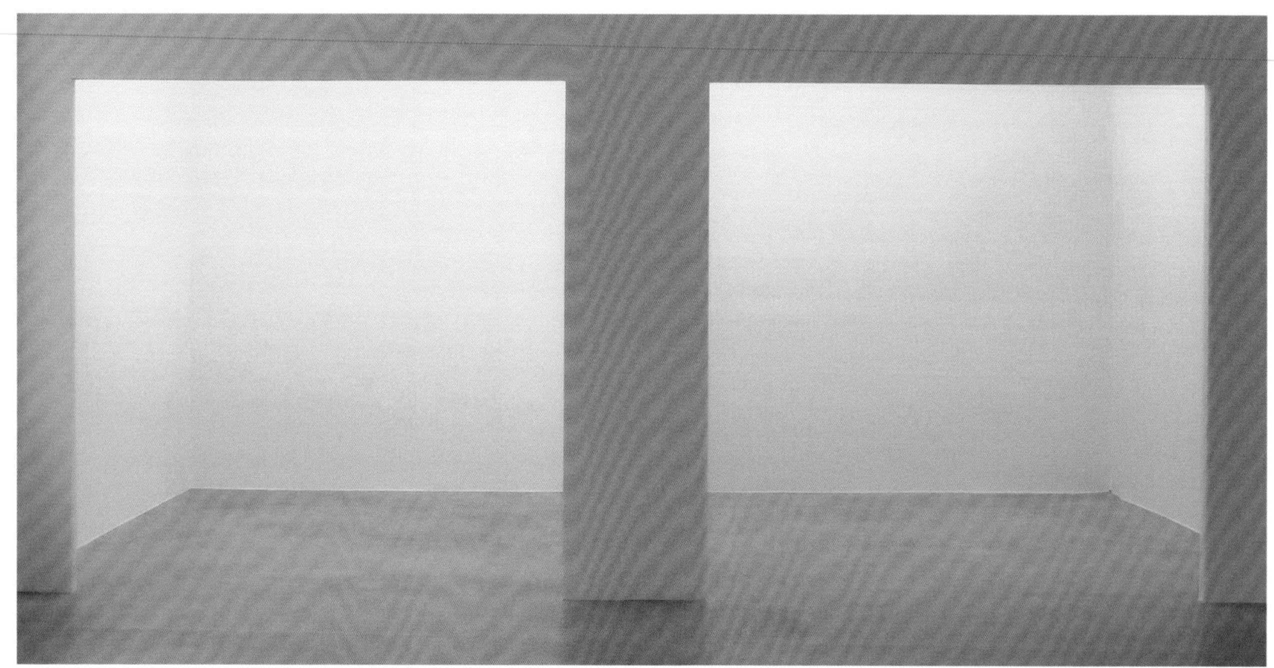

Front and back images of Finch's *West (Sunset in my Motel Room, Monument Valley, February 26, 2007, 5.36-6.06 PM)* subvert expectations of what there is to see in his projects. By turning the screens to face the wall, the artist prevented viewers from looking at the monitors and drew their attention to light from the screens as it illuminated the backdrop of his installation.

facing the wall. The colours of light bouncing off the wall were created by film stills from *The Searchers*, a 1956 Western directed by John Ford. The installation was Finch's attempt to re-create the sunset as it slowly vanished beyond the desert landscape visible from his room. As the name suggests, the location was Monument Valley, Utah, a place that Finch visited on his travels. He measured the colour and intensity of the light as it shifted from warm daylight yellows to pinks, purples and, finally, the deep blues of darkness. He transposed his measurements into CIE chromaticity coordinates, which situate the colour spectrum in relation to the human eye and three-dimensional space. After matching his results to colours in thousands of Ford's film stills, Finch created a subjective replication of the sky at sunset.

The labour and complexity of a project aimed at what is essentially the production of coloured light on a blank wall may seem ludicrous. A kind of madness does exist in projects by Spencer Finch. He uses intense examinations of transient phenomena or past events to accentuate present experiences. Colour becomes a medium for imprinting memory into viewers' minds, allowing them to feel what Finch felt. If only we could re-create the heavenly constellations as they appeared during the Trojan War, or see the light in the sky over Troy, perhaps we could know how Achilles felt as he gazed into the darkness overhead and yearned for success *(The Shield of Achilles, Night Sky Over Troy, 2009)*. These kinds of questions are both whimsical and literary, but what sets Finch apart from other artists is his belief in the science of the act required to produce art. If the precision of making a work – the colour metering and calibration, the data collection, the pixellation – is lost or diminished in the end result, such depletion may be irrelevant. What Finch gives us, though not an authentic recollection of Whitman meeting Lincoln or of his boat trip on the Hudson, is a new experience based on reality as he feels it.

Seasonal Spectrums

An exquisitely landscaped garden by Piet Oudolf emphasizes seasonal variations that enable an experience of colours developing and decaying over time.

Photography Courtesy of Piet Oudolf, Courtesy of Friends of the High Line and Kristof Acke

Piet Oudolf designs and creates both public and private gardens; an example of the latter is this garden in West Cork, Ireland.

'Can you smell the grass?' asks Piet Oudolf, as he walks along a meandering garden path lined with an overflowing haze of wispy blond *Sporobolus* grass. Every now and then, we note fragrant hints of a faint earthy sweetness with underlying notes of coriander and, perhaps, soap. The subtle colours, movement, sound and scent of the tall grass – a smell not at all like the intense green odour that most of us associate with our freshly mown lawns – in combination with the rather untamed feel of the garden, trigger the sense of being in a natural environment. But, as we are soon to learn, all is not as it seems.

Colour and structure

Oudolf's private garden in Hummelo, the Netherlands, is a carefully landscaped composition of textures, colours and structures. When we visit in early autumn, a time during which most conventional gardens are starting to be cut back after the flowering season, Oudolf's oasis is still in full swing. Surrounded by a series of undulating wall-height hedges, his circular garden beds noticeable, from the light delicate clouds of blond *Deschampsia* and its feathery beige cousins to the sharper, red-tipped 'Shenandoah' switch grass. Small groups of *Echinops* – with dark-brown, skeletal stems and spiky, globate seed heads – stand peacefully amidst it all.

The garden serves as something of an experimental laboratory, as many of the plantings Oudolf uses for his projects all over the world are found here. To support the experimentation, in 1982 Oudolf and his wife, Anja, established a nursery on the grounds. For nearly three decades they have been cultivating plants here – many of North American origin – and have bred over 70 new varieties.

Compositions in time

Picking up a branch of seed heads from the *Baptisia* plant, Oudolf explains: 'This plant has white flowers in the summer but looks even better in the autumn, with its black seed heads. In winter, you can hear the seeds rattle inside the pod.' He points out an elegant cluster of *Baptisia* stems,

'Flowers have colour. But if the colour is all you see, it doesn't speak to you'

feature sculptural combinations of perennials and ornamental grasses of differing heights. At this moment, the array of colours is eye-catchingly diverse. And the colours in these compositions are not confined to flowers, as is the case in many traditional gardens. 'I think flowers are more than colour,' Oudolf comments. 'Flowers have colour. But if the colour is all you see, it doesn't speak to you.' Colour in itself is not what makes the garden; what colour needs, he stresses, is structure. 'Colour needs structure to carry it; without colour on something, it's just colour.'

Viewing the garden, we see that the spectrum of the foliage ranges from a furry, silvery green to an intense dark red. The flowers include fine sprinklings of blue *Lobelia* and fading purple balls of fluffy *Allium* balancing on thin green stems. Reds and pinks predominate in this autumn garden, particularly in the bold red blooms of the swamp hibiscus; the drooping pink petals of *Echinacea*, punctuated with pointy black centres; and groups of elongated, hot-pink, furry *Pennisetum* blossoms. Impressive mounds of grasses are especially whose vertical silhouettes make a striking contrast to the fineness of the grass. Soon the stems will glisten frosty white, as winter creeps into the garden.

Oudolf's creations include gardens featured at the Architecture Biennale in Venice; an extensive rooftop project in Chicago's Millennium Park; and an acclaimed planting design for High Line, a city park on a site formerly occupied by an abandoned elevated rail line that once served Lower Manhattan. Each project illustrates the passage of time and highlights the beauty of the natural cycle of growth and decay. Oudolf's gardens are 'compositions in time' that reserve a major role for the seasons. 'I always say brown is a colour. There's beauty even in dead flowers or stems or skeletons or seed heads. Once you accept that, you start thinking differently – not only about flowering time, but also about how to develop things through the seasons.' Thus colour is of the essence the whole year through.

'Seasons are a big part of everyone's life,' he continues. 'Can you imagine a garden that exists →

Another of Oudolf's creations was a garden for visitors to the 2010 Venice Biennale, where he also showed drawings and sketches, such as those pictured here.

An image of the High Line, an abandoned elevated rail line on the west side of Manhattan, before it was converted into a park.

The planting design for the High Line was inspired by the self-seeded landscape that continued to grow on the disused rails for 25 years after trains stopped running.

Sketch of the High Line project.

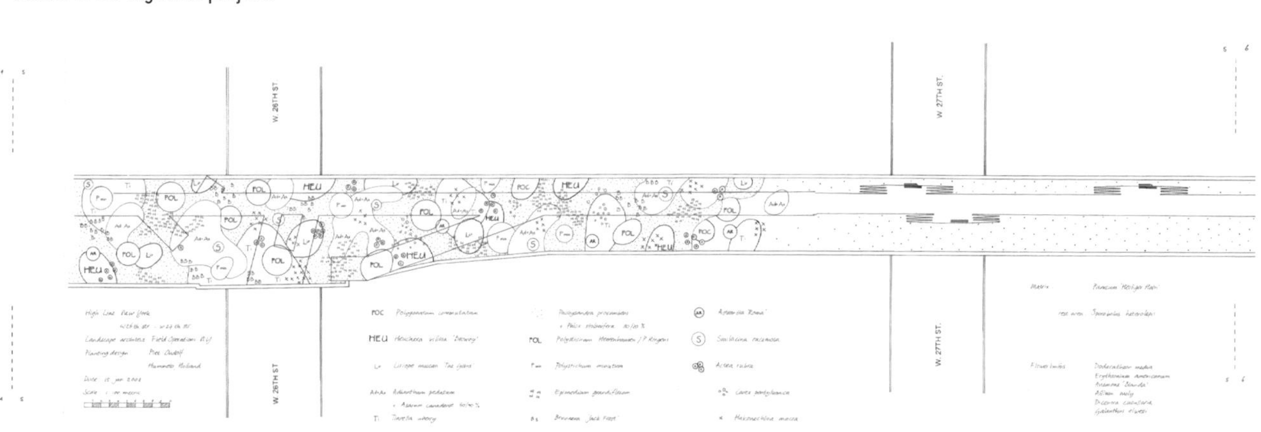

'These gardens become landscapes; they're more than just gardens'

The 210 species of perennials, grasses, shrubs and trees in Section 1 were chosen for their hardiness, sustainability and variation in texture and colour. This project illustrates Oudolf's preference for native species.

'Can you imagine a garden that exists for only one season?'

Completed in 2005, the 1.6-hectare Battery Bosque in New York City features 5575 m² of new perennial gardens.

for only one season, so that when you walk through it in September everything is gone? Gardens exist by emphasizing the seasons, even winter.' Conventionally, we often picture the non-flowering time of year as a lifeless phase. Colour appears only in bursts of blossoms in spring or summer. Oudolf has a more holistic view. 'A garden is for four seasons. It's life and death throughout the seasons, a life cycle in one year. Some things are dying; others are coming alive. That's what makes it so attractive; it's a performance in time.'

The chosen ones

In these gardens, 'plants are performers', each fulfilling a different role according to season, context, climate and soil conditions. For example, some plants shine as soloists in the foreground, while others recede as fillers into the background. Some are chosen for their mass or verticality, some for their accent colours, some for their ability to accentuate surrounding colours. Each has its individual character, 'much like people'. Plants are selected with care, not only for colour and structure but also for sculptural and textural qualities: how they move in the wind (a consideration for Battery Park, which borders New York Harbour), how they freeze, how they catch the light and, most importantly, how they age through the seasons. In most cases, Oudolf uses perennials to produce a sense of dynamism, as these plants die and grow back within a year. Season by season, different plants showcase various parts of the garden by blooming or by changing in colour or form.

One example of a useful garden perennial is *Echinacea,* a slender, medicinal plant with flowers in shades of vivid pink, red, purple and white. 'It flowers for a long time. The seed heads are interesting, and in the end the whole plant turns black,' Oudolf explains. '*Echinacea* can be used in small groups or in masses, and the plant's shape contrasts well with other plants.' Grasses, too, have a diversity of functions. Often used in masses, they provide a spectrum of stunning hues that change throughout the year. They range from several exceptionally tall species, often used to demarcate a garden's more intimate zones, to the extremely light and feathery types, which resemble ethereal clouds of mist. When experienced all together, plants arranged in a well-considered and skilfully composed layout – an arrangement of textures, colours, fragrances and forms – appeal to our emotions more than we realize.

Standing in Oudolf's garden, we experience a sense of movement, contrast, change and, simultaneously, balance and harmony. 'The dynamism of the garden lies in watching it change in front of your eyes. A garden is never complete or perfect. I always see what I want to change next year.' Oudolf laughs before continuing. He believes a garden has qualities that extend beyond its immediate confines. 'These gardens become landscapes. They're more than just gardens. They create moments that remind you of nature, but I don't mean that the garden is a metaphor for nature. Not at all. But it reminds you deeply of nature. It connects with your soul.'

Oudolf's planting in the Chicago Millennium Park's Lurie Garden.

Using analog and digital techniques, Jaap Scheeren and Hans Gremmen experimented with the possibility of creating a three-dimensional colour separation.

cmyk Separations

Dutch photographer Jaap Scheeren and graphic designer Hans Gremmen created a three-dimensional colour separation of an image of a bouquet of flowers.

Photography **Jaap Scheeren**

‘We wanted to create a perfect reproduction without using the computer, but we knew it would be impossible’

The bouquets were photographed separately before being reassembled in Photoshop to reproduce the original image.

Fake Flowers in Full Colour forms part of an ongoing investigation by photographer Jaap Scheeren and graphic designer Hans Gremmen into the use of printing techniques in image-making. A recent manifestation of their experimentation explored the process of creating a colour separation - where a printed image is split into its individual parts of cyan, magenta, yellow and black (CMYK) - from a three-dimensional perspective. They chose a still life of artificial flowers for the project and opted for a combination of analog and digital techniques.

To get this 'thinking exercise' off the ground, Scheeren and Gremmen photographed the flowers and used Photoshop to make the first colour separation. The pair now had four digital images with which to make 'analog' separations of the still life, a task that involved re-creating four identical bouquets and hand-painting the flowers in each image to match those in the corresponding Photoshop version. After photographing each of the bouquets, they assembled all four analog layers in Photoshop to reproduce a single image.

But the story isn't over. 'For a long time,' says Gremmen, 'we called that result our "end image", but a year later, after discussing it again, we felt it wasn't right to have the computer complete the last step in this analog process.' At that point they decided to print the image in offset in 16 layers (four times full colour); in other words, they printed the cyan bouquet in full colour, superimposed the image on that of the magenta bouquet, and so on.

The project evolved into a book, which Gremmen says 'is designed in such a way that one never gets a real grip on the complete images'. And did the experiment succeed? 'Ideally, we wanted to create a perfect reproduction without using the computer. At the same time, we knew it was impossible to get it perfect. But we were curious to see just how close we could get to making a three-dimensional colour separation.'

A photographic still life featuring artificial flowers was deconstructed in Photoshop to reveal its individual CMYK parts. The resulting separations were translated into four identical bouquets, which were painted by hand to match the digital images.

Fake Flowers in Full Colour appears in a book which highlights the experimental nature of the project.

Fabrics

the fabric is half the fashion

Crafted simultaneously by technology and by hand, the artisanal textiles embellished by Jakob Schlaepfer display colours in all their facets.

Photography **Heinz Bigler, Patrick Fuchs, Peter Kaeser and Michael Rast**

Using postcards, digital printing and a library of colours and textiles, Jakob Schlaepfer's Martin Leuthold comes up with vividly coloured and luxuriously textured fabrics that combine intuition, handicraft and the latest technological developments.

Postcards from art director Martin Leuthold's extensive collection – collated to convey moods and themes – form the conceptual starting point of each season's collection.

'Such beautiful yellows are available at the moment – the biggest spectrum possible with ink jet'

One of the latest textiles developed by Swiss manufacturer Jakob Schlaepfer is a sumptuous machine-embroidered fabric aglitter with an amazing 900,000 sequins per metre. According to the textile company's art director, Martin Leuthold, the heaviness of the textured fabric gives the impression of an animal hide, and thanks to newly developed double-sided sequins, simply stroking the cloth in different directions changes both the colour and the pattern. Another innovation Leuthold unveils is a sheer, light-as-a-feather, double-sided fabric: fused to one side is a fine layer of metallic gauze, and the opposite side is digitally printed. In daylight, the fabric looks shiny and metallic, and a black background reveals a vivid, photorealist, floral print. It's enough to make fashion minds work overtime, and even non-fashion minds go weak in the knees at the sight of such exquisite textiles. Christian Lacroix calls Jakob Schlaepfer 'almost a couture house in itself, almost an extension of my design studio'.

Characterized by colour, print and technique, the fabrics made by Jakob Schlaepfer are grounded in an age-old industry that in the early 20th century made St Gallen an international epicentre of textile. At that time, St Gallen produced about half the world's embroidered fabrics. 'St Gallen is built on textiles,' says Leuthold, adding that his company has '800 years of textile tradition' to back its ever-advancing innovations. Founded in 1904, Jakob Schlaepfer plays an integral role in the town's history, pioneering technology that continues today, including the introduction of computers to its operations (1968), the development of thermofixable paste gems in collaboration with Swarovski (1975), and the acquisition of a world patent for sequin production on shuttle embroidery machines (1963) and another patent for a transfer application machine (1983). The development of metallic fabrics followed a decade later. The base fabrics are not manufactured in the company's headquarters; they are sourced from around the world but both printed and embellished in St Gallen. The company has been printing digitally since 2001, but today's cutting-edge technology is a new method of ink-jet printing that goes beyond feeding flat pieces of fabric into a printer, like paper, and allows the manufacturer to print patterns on textured and/or sequinned fabric. 'In the future, you will be able to print the pattern straight onto a dress,' says Leuthold.

Hands-on colour

Jakob Schlaepfer is renowned as a laboratory for textiles, a reputation clearly visible in the design atelier, a beehive of activity where walls and floor are covered with experimental fabrics and print-outs. 'It's a big chaos in here!' Leuthold laughs. 'But amidst this chaos, we find order.' The designers are testing photorealist prints with sequinned fabrics and embellishing laser-cut textiles. Lying on the cutting table is a series of postcards arranged by theme and colour palette. Larger fabric samples hang on the wall. Some of these works in progress will make the final cut; others will not. Everywhere you look, colour, print and texture bring the textiles to life, delighting the eye.

The process of obtaining colours and producing the fabrics is a curious mix of low- and high-tech activities, combining intuition, handicraft and the latest technologies. Each collection begins with Leuthold's postcards. 'I've been collecting postcards for 40 years,' he says, 'while travelling and visiting museums and galleries.' Paintings, works of art and flowers are some of his favourite subjects. Four times a year, the postcards are pulled out at the beginning of each season's design process for two *haute-couture* and two *prêt-à-porter* collections. Because fashion designers select fabrics from these collections for their own seasonal collections, the manufacturer and the designers work in seasonal opposition to each other: Jakob Schlaepfer launches spring/summer collections while the designers are presenting their autumn/winter collections. (If you *really* want to know what's going to be in fashion, take a look at the latest fabrics.)

About 250 new designs are created each season, some in four to six colourways. 'Prints have to change each season, and designers want their own prints. In the past we made only two prints per season, but now it's around 250.' The change to ink-jet printing from screen and marble printing →

made the cost of prints less expensive, and digital techniques simplified the production of a greater number of prints as well as colours. Although fabric designs are rarely created on commission, they are developed with specific labels in mind; Jakob Schlaepfer's clients include Chanel, Dior, Marc Jacobs, Givenchy and Vivienne Westwood. In a sense, the fabric determines the fashion, but it's a symbiotic process: fashion and trends also have an influence on fabric designs. In the words of Yves Saint Laurent: 'The fabric is half the fashion.' Approximately 60 per cent of each fabric collection designed is actually sold.

In preparation for the summer's *haute-couture* collection – which calls for a sense of lightness, graphic black-and-white motifs, and a vivid ethnic palette – Leuthold picks up a postcard of a medieval painting of a nude woman holding a delicate, sheer fabric. He draws a comparison to the sample of an impossibly light, silvery textile made in Japan, which he tosses into the air. 'This is a polyester fabric similar to that used for water filters; it weighs five grams per metre. It's perfect for a theme that emphasizes airiness, feathers and summer skies. We will balance the lightness by adding some weight to the fabric.' Other postcards relevant to the theme, combined with fabric samples dyed in a wide spectrum of colours, are all he needs to come up with a palette of fresh, diaphanous pastels. 'It's about creating stories around colour.' Postcards and samples form the foundation of the designs. Reams of folders lining open shelves are filled with fabric swatches arranged by colour: a single colour in all its many variations. 'We collect colours in this library. We take the colours straight from the textiles and also from the postcards. The colours are not direct copies of what we find in paintings or images but interpretations.'

Taking another postcard, this time showing a historical painting of an Indian nobleman, Leuthold flips through a folder of yellow samples and selects two shades in different materials (one pale, the other almost fluorescent) inspired by the scene's vibrant colours. These samples will be attached to the fabrics that are sent to be dyed.

'Colour used on different scales can change how a fabric is perceived'

Bold and whimsical prints become feature panels fashioned from fabrics designed for the company's interior collection.

In addition to fabrics with subtler, more delicate patterns, the company also specializes in photorealistic prints that demand attention through a colourful explosion of blossoms or graphic tile motifs.

The process of deciding which colours to use is surprisingly hands-on, and the deftness with which he handles the colour and material samples is undeniable evidence of the part Leuthold plays in the decision-making. 'We like light, pretty colours – transparent, watery. But we're also fond of bright, bold, photorealist prints.'

How have colours developed since Leuthold joined the company in 1973? 'Colours have become brighter through the years. This is due mostly to the evolution of electronic media, as currently we work only with digital printing. The ink determines the colours now. Such beautiful yellows are available at the moment – the biggest spectrum possible with ink jet.' Colour, he explains, looks different on different materials. 'Each fabric needs a unique colour, so you can't have a general colour card for each season. The same red can't be used for chiffon, silk, wool, lace and so on. They all take colour in different ways.' Solid colours are hard to re-create in fabric. He mentions green and blue. 'In nature, blue – during the day, at night, in the sky and sea – is nearly always transparent. When you try to transfer this transparency to a fabric with ink or dye, it becomes flat.'

Three-dimensional colour

Besides the basic colour of the fabric and the print, extra colour can be added in the form of embroidery and embellishments such as feathers, pearls, rhinestones and acrylic cutouts. When combined with laser-cut designs, fringes or ruffles, a piece of coloured fabric has a three-dimensional effect. In these complex fabric designs, handicraft and machine meet, as when a machine-embroidered border of ballerinas is hand-finished with tulle tutus, for example, or an oversized laser-cut lace is bejewelled by hand with rhinestones or hand-folded, machine-cut flowers. Embroidery is also hand-programmed into the computer (with all stitches painstakingly counted), and in cases where the machine misses something, the fabric is repaired by hand.

With all fabrics, a sense of dynamism is created by using contrast. Light fabrics such as tulle and polyester are given weight by adding thick →

Day and night, the Jakob Schlaepfer design studio is abuzz with experiments relating to colour, print, texture and material.

embroidery or rhinestones, or by being combined with heavy brocades. Matte fabrics are paired with shiny embellishments, and translucent textiles are interspersed with opaque details. A traditional lace motif can be renewed by stitches made with a contemporary fluorescent or metallic thread. Particularly in the detailing of embellishments and prints, the amount of shine and colour can be explored to achieve special effects. 'Colour used on different scales can change how a fabric is perceived,' Leuthold comments.

Since 1993 the company's exquisite fabrics made for the fashion industry have been translated to serve the interior market. Jakob Schlaepfer's textiles for the interior, which hang in the lobby of the atelier, are clearly influenced by the glamour of the fashion world. The main difference is that fabrics used for interiors – such as wall coverings, curtains and upholstery – require a greater degree of durability and are somewhat subtler in colour. 'Fashion exerts a big influence on interiors nowadays,' our guide continues. 'But colours for the latter are chosen more carefully, since interiors are meant to last longer – you can change clothes every day. So it's best not to have too much colour in interiors and to use it more as a highlight or in accessories that are easy to change.' Photorealist floral prints, for instance, work well as feature wall panels, and boldly patterned curtain fabrics become sleek abstract stripes when the curtains are pulled back. Embellishments remain, however, even in cases of neutral colours, when fabrics display embroidery, sequins, crystals or a metallic sheen. Craftsmanship is a given: the firm's Korsakow curtain is composed of embossed cubes of foam tipped with gold leather and applied by hand to transparent tulle. Leuthold explains that it's easy to get tired of prints and colours when they have been part of the same space for too long. And the easiest way to determine this? 'We test all interior fabrics by hanging them around the office. If they bore us rather quickly, we know!'

Despite the wide range of fabrics produced by Jakob Schlaepfer, one leitmotif remains constant

Heavily sequinned fabrics aglitter with up to 900,000 sequins per metre bring to mind the skins of shimmering creatures. Stroking the surface of such a fabric – especially one with double-sided sequins – changes its colour and pattern.

Designers such as Vivienne Westwood, Alexander McQueen and Izeta have used Jakob Schlaepfer fabrics in their spectacular catwalk collections.

'The same red can't be used for chiffon, silk, wool, lace and so on. They all take colour in different ways'

across all collections: sequins, the house speciality. Every imaginable sequinned adornment in every possible colour is made here. A small selection includes sequin-bordered ruffles, patterns embroidered with sequins, tassels (machine-stitched onto a layer of structural paper, sequins become a string of tassels when the paper is removed) and lace composed entirely of stitched sequins. What attracts designers to sequins? 'They are glamorous, shiny and three-dimensional. And because all sequins once had to be sewed to the fabric by hand, they are a reminder of traditional craftsmanship.'

The sequin sample book contains a seemingly endless assortment of sequins: antique, double-sided, velvety, glow-in-the-dark, glossy, transparent, embossed and more. Sequins can even be printed with the same pattern used for the fabric. In two minutes, a sample of white sequinned fabric fed into the ink-jet printer is adorned with a vividly printed still life featuring flowers. The same coloured pattern may look completely different when printed on different types of white sequins – matte, semi-opaque, iridescent or holographic. It is through constant experimentation and reinvention that each season Jakob Schlaepfer keeps designers on their toes with a tacit reminder: the past influences each step towards the future, and the sky's the limit.

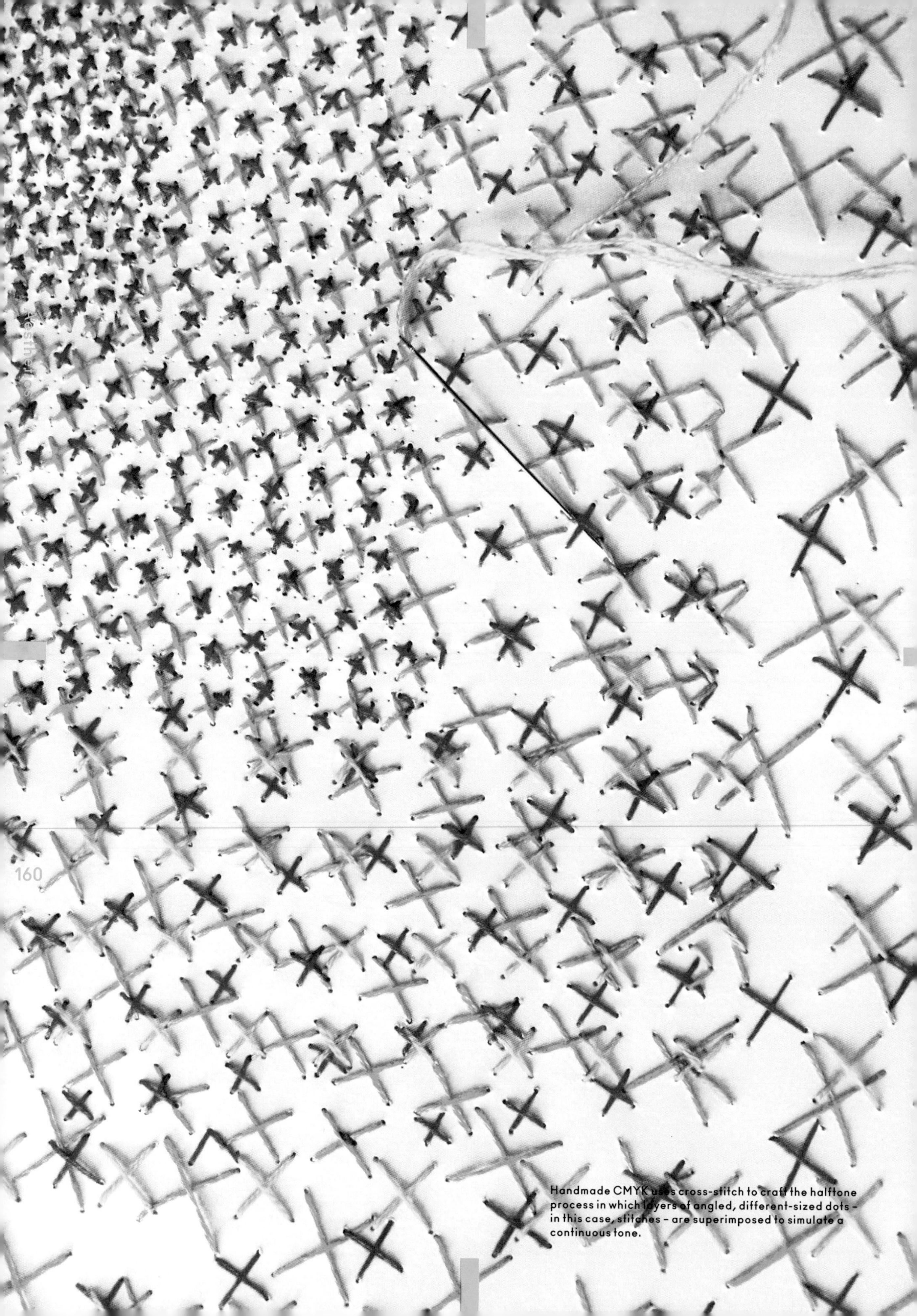

Handmade CMYK uses cross-stitch to craft the halftone process in which layers of angled, different-sized dots – in this case, stitches – are superimposed to simulate a continuous tone.

Graphics

tactile tints

Estonian-born, London-based artist and designer Evelin Kasikov combines print technology and craft to deconstruct colour and make print a tactile experience.

Photography **Evelin Kasikov**

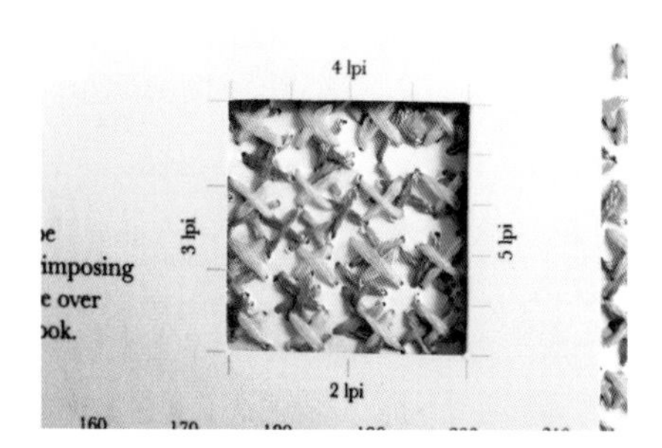

Evelin Kasikov's stitches represent the cyan, magenta, yellow and black halftone dots that overlap to reproduce any colour desired. The resolution achieved by Handmade CMYK varies between two to five lines per inch.

Behind the screen: colour 'deconstructs' as print technology is translated into tactile graphics.

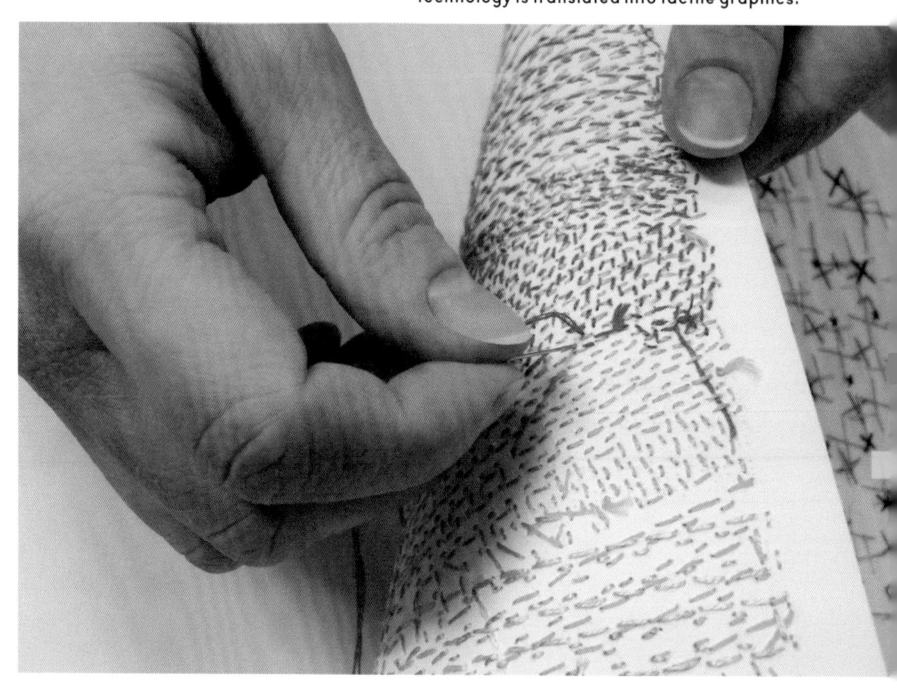

In exploring the potential of the printed page, Evelin Kasikov experimented with techniques for transforming print technology into a handmade form of art. Although Kasikov is influenced by craft and materials, her work has an analytic edge that is grounded in the context of graphic design. Her experiments with colour-reproduction methods combined with embroidery eventually led to the technique she calls Handmade CMYK. 'This project is about experiencing visual messages through handmade graphics. I was working with the idea of tactile print, and my aim was to add another dimension to it,' says Kasikov. 'A page from a book is flat, but I wondered what would happen if you could see inside a colour – if you could even touch the inner structure of colour?'

Handmade CMYK translates halftone dots into cross-stitch. The halftone process (in the four-colour CMYK colour model) works like this. Layers of different-sized dots are superimposed to simulate a continuous tone: from a distance, our eyes register this pattern of dense halftone dots as a field of colour: the smaller the dots, the lighter the colour. Screens used to print the dots are positioned at different angles (cyan 105, magenta 75, yellow 90 and black 45) to create a combined halftone pattern that can reproduce any colour. Dots are represented by angled, overlapping stitches in cyan, magenta, yellow and black cotton thread. The number of strands used determines the intensity of the colour. The angled dot screens become cross-stitch screens, which are printed with the desired dot pattern and transferred to fabric that can be embroidered. The resolution of a halftone screen is measured in the number of lines per inch: the higher the resolution, the more detailed the image. The resolution achieved by Handmade CMYK falls between two and five lines per inch.

Kasikov hopes to redefine familiar techniques – both handcrafted and computer-generated – by revealing the process that leads to the construction of an image. Handmade CMYK is cross-stitch for the 21st century.

'I wondered what would happen if you could see inside a colour and even touch its inner structure'

The colour intensity of the stitched halftone dots is determined by the angle and size of the stitches, and by the number of individual strands used.

Natural Dyes

Painted by Nature

With design and fashion focusing increasingly on authenticity and the environment, there's a new appreciation for the irregular beauty of natural colorants.

Photography Joost van Brug, Peter Cuypers, Courtesy of Formafantasma, Stefanie Gratz, Courtesy of Raw Color, Peter Stigter, Studio Claudy Jongstra and Roel van Tour

Juice is extracted from all manner of vegetables – carrots, beetroot, cabbage – by design studio Raw Color, which uses the natural fluid to create vibrant inks for printing and dyeing textiles.

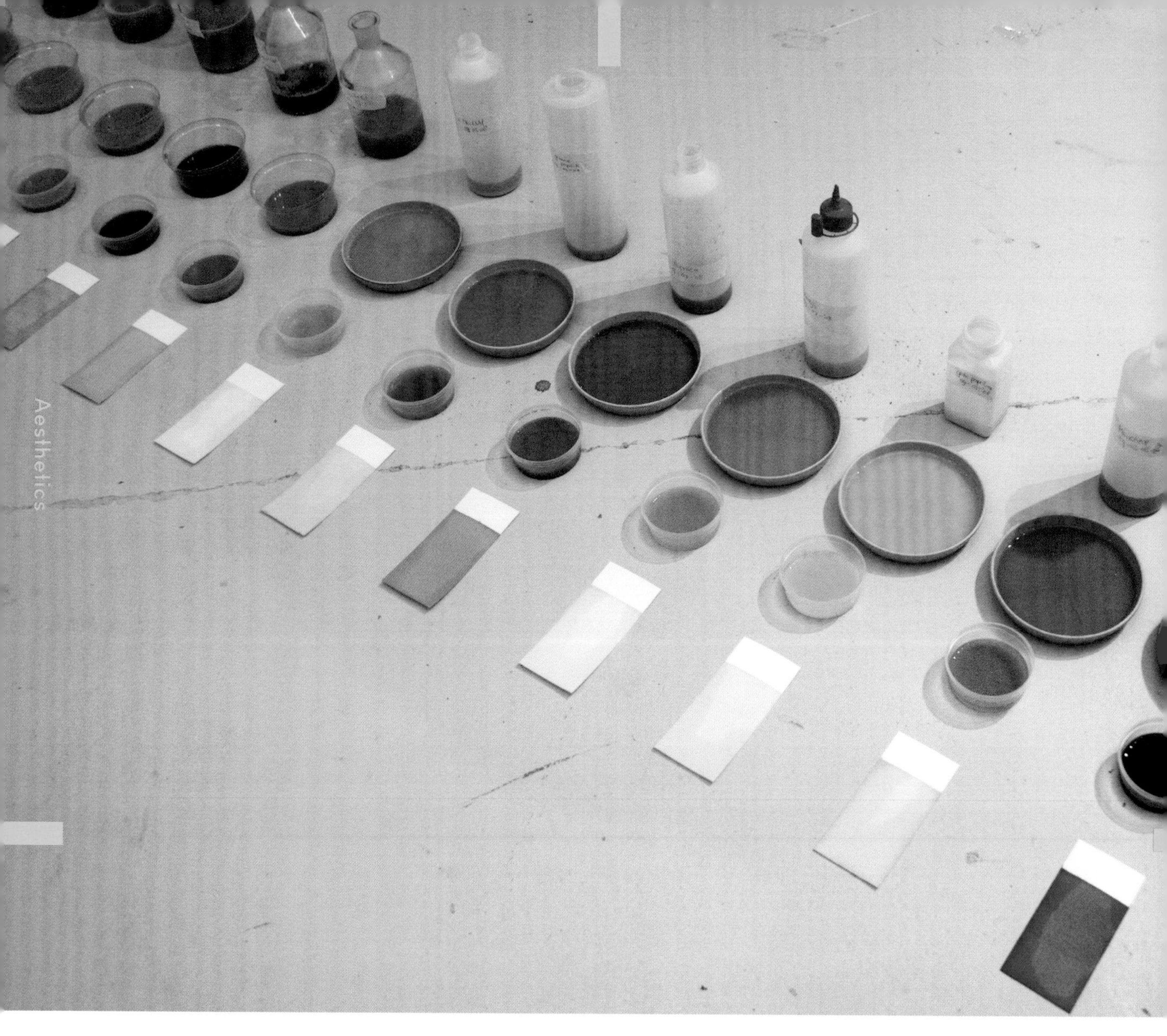

The harvested vegetable colours are captured by a new process preserving their intensity on colour cards.

Beetroot, pumpkin, cabbage, carrot, radish: if it's a vegetable, Raw Color have put it in the juicer to make ink

As long as colour has been used for decoration, natural dyestuffs have been part of the process. For millennia and across civilizations, plants (wild and cultivated), minerals and animal life (such as insects and molluscs) have been dried, crushed, infused and fermented in all sorts of ways to create the pigments and dyes that enrich our lives. Think textiles, paint, cosmetics and food. Down through the ages, natural dyestuffs have contributed to economic and cultural trade among nations, while encouraging biodiversity in the natural landscape. Only 150 years ago, all dyes were natural: some of the better-known dyestuffs were indigo (leaves) for blue; madder (root) for pinks, browns and reds; and cochineal (insect) for carmine. In terms of geography, many colours were named after the location of their origins, meaning that *terroir* applied to colour as much as to wine.

In the 19th century, the Industrial Revolution shifted the focus to synthetic colorants, which transformed the accessibility, quality, consistency, quantity and efficiency of colour used in large-scale manufacturing. It became easier to produce colour – certainly it's less difficult to mix up a purple pigment in a laboratory than to make it by extracting mucus from a Murex snail – rendering previously exclusive colours more affordable. The ability to synthesize colour meant its production was no longer restricted by a constituent raw material. The science of colour flourished, opening the door for new industries and fashion trends. Natural colour retreated into the hands of specialized artisans and cottage industries.

The recent revival of natural colour comes as no coincidence, linked as it is to the international call for environmental and ethical responsibility across all sectors. The urgency for cultural preservation in a globalized world – UNESCO supports ethnic traditions of natural dyeing in its cultural programme – and the longing for authenticity in design have aided the cause. In this respect, ancient traditions can provide inspiration for the future, and modern technology can be used to update preindustrial techniques and materials with a strong connection to nature and craftsmanship. Gradually, colours can retire from the →

A series of photographs illustrates the proportions of vegetables present in a particular ink – the ink analysed here is one-third pumpkin and two-thirds red cabbage.

Categorized by shades and families a new colour map is created which shows their beautiful diversity.

Using the flax from a Dutch farmhouse Meindertsma created her new collection Flax.

'It's exciting, because no two colours are ever precisely the same'

Common Madder, Rubia Tinctorium, is used to colour the wool red.

The prototype of the Urchin poufs were coloured with vegetable dyes.

Christien Meindertsma knitting a rug for her Aran collection.

Christien Meindertsma's uses wool of Dutch and New Zealand sheep for a lot of her designs.

laboratory and find sources within the natural environment. Let's look at some of the movers and shakers who are helping natural colour to reach the forefront of design and fashion.

The colourists

One of only a few natural-dye houses in the United States, Noon Design Studio uses sustainably harvested pigments and dyes for adding colour to clothes and accessories. Founded by textile designer Jane Palmer in 2010, the Los Angeles-based studio takes a local approach to colour: 'The pigments I use include indigo and earth minerals found mainly in the southern Appalachian region of the United States, where I'm from. The dyes, which are from all around the world, come mainly from different parts of plants – including flowers, bark, wood, leaves and roots – plus a few insects. Each dye I use is indigenous to a specific area, and where possible I try to obtain the materials directly from the farmer.' Palmer also mentions bougainvillea, a dye-producing plant that is locally harvested for its brilliant colour. 'People think that natural dyes are either brown or yellow. Whenever I show the range of colours I can make, people are astonished. Natural dyes produce an amazing luminosity of colour. The textile ceases to have a surface and instead becomes like a vast night sky full of depth.' She continues by pointing out that the use of natural dyes sometimes goes beyond colour: 'Many people also believe that specific dyes have certain healing properties that can be absorbed through the skin from a naturally dyed garment.'

With over 20 years' experience, Leentje van Hengel – founder of Amsterdam-based dye studio Tinctoria – is one of only a handful of people in the Netherlands working professionally in this field. Her custom-dyed fabrics, for which she uses some ten natural dyestuffs, are intended for the fashion and design industries. Interestingly, natural dyes work best with natural materials like silk, wool, linen, and bamboo – and have an aversion to synthetics. According to Van Hengel, practising to perfect natural dyeing techniques has been challenging, but the result is 'slow colour' at its finest. 'Controlling the production of natural colour is definitely more complex. Different processes create different colours, which can be sensitive to changes in temperature, acidity and so on – not to mention the way that various materials react differently to the same dye. Controlling the process is definitely a craft in itself!' Nontoxic mordants are employed where needed, for colour and light fastness; stringently checked, the dye effluent is safe enough to pour down the drain. On the bright side, a complex process produces complex colours: 'The colours are definitely different, rounder, more vibrant. They're not weak – that's for sure.' Van Hengel explains that a naturally dyed textile also needs extra attention in the wash to prevent fading, implying careful treatment for a product that will not be discarded easily.

Designers using natural colour

While some designers use natural dyes simply for their colours, others explore their qualities in a more conceptual context. For a series of Urchin Poufs, Dutch product designer Christien Meindertsma worked with Tinctoria to dye the wool required for the project. 'For the research into this series, we looked for plants and trees that grow in Europe,' says Meindertsma. 'We used →

buckthorn, walnut, chestnut, weld, madder, woad, sage and sorghum.' With her strong focus on craftsmanship and the journey that (natural) materials undergo to become products, she saw the use of natural dyes as a natural step. 'I'm interested in working with natural dyes because their sources can be grown, which means we're talking about renewable products,' she continues. Not only are the resulting colours vivid and playful; they also complement the natural material. 'It's exciting, because no two colours are ever precisely the same.'

For Dutch fashion designer Jan Taminiau, the choice of madder-dyed fabrics for Evolution, his SS/08 collection, was an easy one. 'The colour in this collection has a purpose. We wanted the colour to be able to change easily and to age by light. We discovered that the natural technique had this quality.' The collection comprises nine looks that evolve in style and colour, highlighting the stunning nuances of madder and fully revealing its beauty: madder can produce over 20 colours. As the fabric in Taminiau's design for 'the woman' turns a shade darker, transforming from a nude to a sun-beaten pink, the cloth in his design for 'the man' shifts from a dark liver to an off-white. The embellishments and detailing alter correspondingly. Here, the potential discoloration of naturally dyed fabrics is a positive quality. 'It's about the subtlety of ageing and creating a sense of

Jan Taminiau's Evolution collection showcases the full spectrum of colours that can be obtained from the madder plant: hues that include delicate pinks, intense reds, earthy browns and delicate beiges.

'Natural dyes produce an amazing luminosity of colour'

something lived in. People normally want a colour to remain the same, but I knew I would lose some colour in this collection – that's what I wanted to happen. It's an evolution in itself.'

Taking colour into their own hands

Alongside using traditional sources of colourants, some designers make colour their own way, in this case inspired by the kitchen. Most people drink vegetable juice, but German/Dutch design duo Raw Color dye and print with it, showcasing its qualities in the purest way possible. Beetroot, pumpkin, cabbage, carrot, capsicum, even radish: if it's a vegetable chances are, it's been through the juicer of Christoph Brach and Daniera ter Haar to make ink. With a strong base in research and experiments combining graphic design and photography, the duo initiated Raw Color which is the name of their studio and the projects involving, among others, vegetable juice. Beginning with a series of posters printed directly by vegetable juice connected to a juicer, their experiment continued to mixing juices to create ink then ink-jet printing and finally dyeing textiles with it. With the precision of juice scientists, the inks are designated colour codes which outline the type of vegetables used and its percentage. For instance 0201 PUM50RCA BC means 50% pumpkin and 50% red cabbage. With ink-jet printing, where regular print cartridges were filled with vegetable juice - C (Red Cabbage), M (Beetroot), Y (Pumpkin) - the qualities of the natural ink influenced the outcome where the irregular juice flow caused a random striped pattern with every print and caused an unexpected problem: 'The vegetable fibres kept getting stuck in the printerhead!' Christoph Brach recalls. The colours also faded less when printed via ink-jet. To retain the colour with their silk textiles (which are dyed in jars for 2-3 days) colour fixing is achieved by vinegar. As with all natural products, the matter of deterioration inevitably arises: 'Some of the juices were starting to get a bit stinky after a while,' Brach laughs. In the end, boiling them did the trick. What were the most surprising vegetables? 'Red cabbage produces many colours from pink to purple and ultramarine depending on if it's mixed with vinegar or on the type of paper. You would expect radish to give pale juice but it's surprisingly bright pink when used as a dye.' Currently investigating the possibility of printing with vegetable inks commercially, the duo demonstrate that they are truly a laboratory for raw colour.

Coloured with vegetables and spices, Formafantasma's Autarchy series looks delectable enough to devour. The Italian studio's tableware is moulded from an 'almost edible' dough that is 70 per cent flour, 20 per cent shredded agricultural waste and 10 per cent natural limestone. 'The use of naturally sourced colour was a direct consequence of the idea of using a flour-based material to create a biodegradable, low-temperature dry clay. We wanted to use easily available materials in our search for an intuitive and immediate way of producing goods,' explains Andrea Trimarchi, one half of Formafantasma. Colours were extracted in the studio. 'We extracted green by boiling vegetables such as spinach in water. For pink, roots like beetroot and rhubarb were immersed in pure spirit. In both cases, we also ground part of the vegetables into the mixture,' continues cofounder Simone Farresin. 'We added the spices – saffron, curcuma, paprika, cinnamon, nutmeg, cocoa and curry – directly to the dough.' Different flours yielded different colours: rye and sorghum flour produced darker shades and highly refined flours lighter tints. 'Basically, we made these dishes colourful and attractive by using almost the same techniques a cook uses in the kitchen.' →

Inspired by methods and materials used in the kitchen, Formafantasma's Autarchy series consists of a flour-based clay that is coloured with vegetable extracts and spices.

From start to finish

Certain designers take specific aspects of colour into their own hands. Others are more interested in the complete picture. Working from her atelier in Spannum, a town in the northern Dutch province of Friesland, felt designer Claudy Jongstra is closely involved in the design and production of her large wall tapestries, which are compositions of woollen felt and materials such as linen and silk. Jongstra uses natural colorants, cultivates some of the plants from which they are sourced, makes her own dyestuffs and tends her own flock of Drenthe Heath sheep. Between the studio and the house is a garden in which she grows 150 species of plants – some on the endangered list – for her experiments with dyes. She says that most of these plants were grown commonly in the past; some were even weeds. Within three months after she planted the garden, it became a haven for butterflies and bees. For Jongstra, colour is more than just dye; it's a symbiosis involving ecology, heritage and humanity.

Jongstra switched to natural colour in 2003, the year in which she clad aluminium shutters in felt for the Lloyd Hotel in Amsterdam and watched as the natural textile rejected the application of synthetic dyes. Tests showed that organic dyes enabled the felt to retain its colour. The reason is simply that natural materials have an affinity for organic dyes and a dislike for the harshness of their synthetic counterparts. 'From that moment on, we stopped using synthetic colour. There was no transition,' Jongstra laughs. 'Now I can live my life only with natural colours.'

Her dyeing room overlooking the garden is where the action happens. Here we find huge dye pots and bags of dried plant material such as onion skins, walnut shells and larkspur. Coloured wool samples hang from a rack, tinted light beige to rich brown using red clover from Jongstra's own harvest. In 2010 Jongstra took self-sufficiency to a new level when she began farming dye-producing plants on a larger scale. Currently three species are being piloted in nearby fields: red clover, larkspur and dandelion.

Jongstra has a keen interest not only in the vivid colours she extracts from natural dyestuffs, but also in how the relationship between colour and people, like the grower of the dye-plants or the designer who applies the colours, affects the intensity of the result. In both cases the closer the connection, the more intense the colour.

'You get the most brightness when you really connect with the colour: this gives colour another dimension. It's like felt-making: if the maker is distracted, it shows in the work.' Jongstra recalls two batches of larkspur that were grown by different farmers: one organically, the other conventionally. One would expect that the organically grown plants would have produced better-quality colour, but this was not the case. 'The wife of the non-organic farmer gave her plants a lot of care and attention, and in the end they produced much richer colour. There is more to natural colour than just planting a seed and following instructions.' Perhaps it has something to do with the primal quality of felt, the oldest type of textile, in combination with the way our eyes immediately feel comforted by natural colour. Jongstra: 'Natural colours just belong.'

Commercial applications

To date, natural colour has been confined largely to small-scale production with an artisanal basis. The increasing need for commercial products made with environmentally friendly materials and techniques will no doubt involve natural colour. Before this happens, however, certain hurdles must be overcome: the laborious process involved, inconsistent results and high costs. 'It's harder to standardize natural colours,' says Jane Palmer. 'People who love naturally dyed fabrics love them for their variations and that one-of-a-kind look, but people who make products for the mass market dislike them for the very same reasons.' Addressing this issue from the perspective of the manufacturer, Dutch company Rubia Pigmenta Naturalia (Rubia for short) developed a water-soluble extract from the madder root for use in industrial applications. 'Industrial dyers want consistency: they want the same today as yesterday as tomorrow,' explains Anco Sneep, Rubia's general manager. 'What they don't want is plant residue stuck in their machinery.' While the colour composition remains identical in each batch of Rubia's extract, the concentration is subject to seasonal variations. Hence the concentration is specified on each packet to enable the user to adjust the amount of dyestuff if needed. Like Jongstra, Rubia controls the whole process to ensure the product stays true to its word: the company owns the plants, oversees their cultivation and runs its own production operation.

Designers got the organic colour ball rolling, but big brands are taking notice – and are increasingly dipping their toes into 'greener' waters. The ever-rising demand for ethical products shows that consumers are spending with their consciences and asking industry to follow suit. Forbo, the world's largest linoleum producer, has worked together with Jongstra to launch the Marmoleum Oxyd collection: flooring in four subtle colours containing only natural oxide pigments. Rubia is collaborating with Stella McCartney to create colours for an upcoming sportswear collection for Adidas. Inspired by its heritage, Japanese fashion sports brand Onitsuka Tiger recently introduced the Aisen collection, which highlights the tradition of indigo dyeing and is to be followed by a collection that explores vegetable dyes. →

Vegetable extracts – including beetroot and spinach – and spices like cinnamon and coffee are added to colour the 'dough' that forms the basis of the edible-looking Autarchy tableware.

Natural colorants work best with natural materials like felted wool, silk and linen, the fabrics with which Claudy Jongstra crafts her striking tapestries. Her pieces hang in public institutions around the world, including the Amsterdam Public Library.

Filled with bags of harvested dye-producing plants and samples of naturally dyed fabrics, Claudy Jongstra's studio overlooks a garden brimming with the beauty of natural colour.

'You get the most brightness when you really connect with the colour'

What all these projects illustrate is a vastly upgraded image of natural colour, which is no longer old-fashioned but sexy, contemporary and chic. Natural colour seems to have the most impact when used together with other natural materials/ techniques to develop a holistic narrative for a product that's been designed with the environment in mind: a complete package, so to speak. No doubt, natural colour will bounce back with a vengeance, but it will take time. Research and development for the mass market, in particular, present more than one complex problem. Forbo design director Josee de Pauw warns that the process leading to an end product is long. 'Vegetable dyes sound appealing, but stringent tests must be conducted first. Will UV light influence the colour? What about regular wear and tear? Where to source the raw materials?' Because natural colours have been largely forgotten since the 19th century, everything about their production, including dyeing, needs to be updated and adapted to the contemporary context. The solutions may not even lie in modern Western society but in far-flung ethnic cultures where age-old dyeing skills are still required for traditional crafts. Delving into archaeology and anthropology may also shed some clues. And closer to home, what's the easiest way to begin? Claudy Jongstra: 'Just do it. Buy a kilo of onions and try it for yourself!'

p

Nature of purple

Purple assumes a special, almost sacred place within nature: flowers in shades of lavender, orchid, lilac, and violet are often delicate and may be considered precious. Purple uplifts, calms the mind and nerves, and offers a sense of spirituality. Because purple is a mix of a strong warm hue and a strong cool hue – red and blue, respectively – it has both warm and cool properties. Surrounding oneself with too much purple can cause moodiness.

Get inspired

Linked to inspiration and relaxation, purple embodies a balance of stimulating red and placid blue. Adding purple to a working environment is beneficial to creativity. Richard Wagner composed his operas in a room featuring shades of violet, his chromatic source of inspiration.

Royal hue

The colour of royalty, purple connotes luxury, wealth and sophistication. Looking for a historical context, we find two Roman emperors – Julius and Augustus Caesar – who both decreed that only the emperor could wear purple. When Nero ascended the throne, the wearing and even the sale of purple became punishable by death. Even today, purple robes are worn by royalty and others in positions of authority.

Purple phrases

A 'purple cow' is something remarkable, eye-catching, unusual. 'Purple prose' denotes exaggerated, highly imaginative writing or even colourful lies. 'Purple speech' refers to profanity. And those in a 'purple haze' are in state of confusion that is possibly drug-induced.

u

r

p

'I think it pisses God off if you walk by the colour purple in a field somewhere and don't notice it.'

Alice Walker

l

'He wrapped himself in quotations – as a beggar would enfold himself in the purple of Emperors.'

Rudyard Kipling

Did you know that

... purple is the bee's favourite colour? More specifically, the European buff-tailed bumblebee (*Bombus terrestris*) prefers violet flowers to blue ones. A study has shown that violet flowers in the vicinity of beehives were far more popular than the insect's second choice: blue blossoms. Bee colonies with access to purple flowers harvested more nectar. Past research has shown that animals often have favourite colours, smells and signals when it comes to choosing a mate, but little research has been done on how such sensory preferences affect searches for food.

... the popularity of purple in Roman times led to the near extinction of the murex family of shellfish? The natural dye of the murex was extracted to produce purple. The dye was very expensive, because it took over 8000 shellfish and a great deal of intensive labour to make a single gram of purple dye.

... the first mass-produced synthetic dye was mauve, a rather pale shade of purple? The dye was discovered, more or less by accident, in 1856 by William Henry Perkin, who called it 'mauveine'. His invention marked the beginning of the chemical and pharmaceutical industry.

... the official name of Beijing's famous 'Forbidden City' is 'The Purple Forbidden City', a reference to a secret purple area of heaven thought to be near the North Star?

... in Thailand purple is worn by a widow mourning her husband's death?

... Leonardo da Vinci believed the power of meditation increases ten times when you're bathed by purple light, such as daylight streaming through purple stained glass?

... if you're born 'in the purple' you are a member of a royal or other high-ranking family?

... early life on earth might have been purple? In 2007 a team of geneticists at the University of Maryland suggested that whereas plants now use chlorophyll to harness the sun's rays, primeval microbes may have used retinal (a form of vitamin A) to photosynthesize. Retinal is a simpler molecule and easier to produce in a low-oxygen environment, such as that which characterized early life on earth. Because retinal absorbs green light and reflects red and violet light, the microbes would have appeared to be purple.

... in 2003 a very odd species of purple frog was found in the Ghat hills of India? *Nasikabatrachus sahyadrensis* ('nose frog from Sahyadra') is a 7-cm-long, dark-purple blob with a pointy snout. It spends its time buried underground feasting on termites, surfacing for only two weeks a year to mate. The males make a loud chicken-like sound. The purple frog is unique; its closest relatives live in the Seychelles, but it split from them more than 130 million years ago.

... purple fruits and vegetables are rich in flavonoids, which are the most abundant and powerful of all the phytochemicals contained in the foods we eat? One of the many categories of flavonoids helps make blood vessels healthier. Purple foods include plums and aubergines, as well as certain types of cabbages and potatoes. Purple food has even rocketed into space. The 'Purple Orchid Three' is a sweet potato now being cultivated in Hainan Province, China, from seeds that were on the nation's Shenzhou VI rocket in 2005.

... February is associated with the colour purple? The birthstone for those born in February is amethyst, which is also a sacred stone for Tibetan Buddhists, who use it to make prayer beads.

... in the United States, the poker chip worth the most ($5000) is purple?

Stay cool

Blue has long possessed a calming effect on the mind. Light, medium and deep blues convey a sense of quietness, clarity and serenity. The soothing quality of blue makes it ideal for pyjamas – an aid to a good night's sleep.

Trust in me

Loyalty and trust are inseparable. Blue is the number-one choice for use in corporate branding. Research has shown that blue is the most popular colour in the world.

Spiritual calling

Blue expresses an air of introspection that is associated with spirituality. The ancient Egyptians chose lapis lazuli to represent the afterlife. Painters have often used blue to represent heaven, and in Christian works of art the Virgin Mary is frequently depicted wearing blue garments.

Stand by me

The tranquillity and permanence of blue is translated into loyalty and faithfulness: a 'true blue' friend remains steadfast, evoking an image of dependability that may also imply conservativeness.

Serve and protect

Navy blue is often associated with authority, law and order: the uniforms of police and military forces worldwide are a good example, as are the many national flags that feature dark blue. Blue has been used as protection against witches, and Egyptian pharaohs wore blue to ward off evil.

Power hungry

In the Christian West, blue emerged in the 12th century. Initially, blue pigments were rare and affordable only to the wealthy, hence the association with aristocracy, royalty and the term 'blue blood'. Prestige ultimately gives rise to power and praise: the award for first prize is a 'blue ribbon'.

Away and beyond

Blue suggests a feeling of distance and is used to show perspective. Symbolically, it communicates a broad vista of the universe beyond these earthly bonds. Adventuring into the unknown is to go 'into the wild blue yonder'.

Speak easy

All shades of blue encourage easy communication, invite contact and promote interaction. Notes written on blue paper are recommended for remembering important information. In certain Eastern religions, blue represents the throat chakra, which enables the expression of thoughts and feelings.

Spick-and-span

The obvious relationship between blue and water also explains the connection between blue and cleanliness. Delving even deeper into this alliance with water, we find a reference to Earth – covered largely by oceans – as the 'Blue Planet'.

Feeling blue

To 'feel blue' is to feel sad. Blue – and especially the darker shades, which may be perceived as cold and melancholy – can convey gloom. In India and Iran, for example, blue is associated with mourning.

l e b u

'Blue colour is everlastingly appointed by the Deity to be a source of delight.'

John Ruskin

Did you know that

... 'to be blue' in German (Blau sein) means 'to be drunk'? This derives from the traditional use of urine (the production of which is stimulated by drinking alcohol, a diuretic) to dissolve the indigo dyestuff needed to make blue textiles.

... blue is an appetite suppressant? Think of how few naturally occurring blue foods exist. Furthermore, our bodies have been finely tuned through the millennia to detect blue warning signs that indicate dangerous foods. To shed pounds, some suggest serving food on blue plates or, better still, dyeing food blue!

... the largest mammal on Earth is the blue whale? The biggest of the species ever recorded measured 34.6 m long – that's around 2.5 bus lengths – and weighed approximately 170 tonnes. At birth, a blue whale weighs between 5 and 7 tonnes and is roughly 6 to 7.6 m long.

... blue ice is old ice.

... mosquitoes are attracted to the colour blue twice as much as to any other colour?

... blue is the colour most preferred by men? A survey has shown blue to be the bestselling colour in women's sweaters, evidently because women realize how much men like blue.

... when your eyes are fully adapted to the dark your range of vision recognizes blue better than red?

... the connection between brides and 'something blue' has been around as long as the wedding ceremony has existed? The present fad for blue garters was preceded by blue worn as a sign of love and fidelity in ancient Rome, and in pre-Victorian times bridal gowns were often blue, denoting purity.

... a year consists of 12 lunar cycles and that a full moon occurs monthly? The term 'blue moon' refers to the extra full moon that appears every two to three years owing to an annual discrepancy of approximately 11 days between the solar and lunar calendars. 'Once in a blue moon' actually happens quite a few times in the span of a life that lasts seven or eight decades.

'I have often said that I wish I had invented blue jeans: the most spectacular, the most practical, the most relaxed and nonchalant. They have expression, modesty, sex appeal, simplicity – all I hope for in my clothes.'

Yves Saint Laurent

g

‘Green represents the dead image of life.’

Rudolf Steiner

r

e

Smart card

A United States Permanent Resident Card is an identification card attesting to the permanent-residence status of an alien living in the United States. It is known informally as a ‘green card’, because it was green from 1946 to 1964 and has been green since May 2010. Between 1965 and 2010, the colour changed regularly to deter forgery.

Green phrases

‘Getting the green light’ indicates approval to proceed with a project or task. Having ‘green fingers’ means being able to make plants grow. When you are ‘green with envy’ you are jealous or envious. And when you ‘turn green’ you appear to be nauseous.

e

Green isn’t so green

Because the colour green is a mix of blue and yellow, it is impossible to dye plastic pure green or to print green ink on paper without contamination. Green is such a difficult colour to manufacture that toxic substances are often used to stabilize it. This means that green plastic and paper cannot be recycled or composted safely, because they could contaminate the environment.

n

Soothing green

Green has a soothing effect on people. It works mentally as well as physically to relax our minds and bodies; to help alleviate depression, nervousness and anxiety; and to generate a sense of renewal, self-control and harmony.

Good things, bad things

Culturally, green has broad and sometimes contradictory implications. In some cultures, green symbolizes hope and growth, and in others green is associated with death, sickness or demons. Muslims, for instance, consider green a sacred colour: green predominates in the flags of Islamic nations, and Muslims wear green turbans after making the pilgrimage to Mecca. But in English-speaking cultures, green is often associated with envy.

‘Sometimes our fate resembles a fruit tree in winter. Who would think that those branches would turn green again and blossom, but we hope it, we know it.’

Johann Wolfgang von Goethe

Did you know that

... medieval brides wore green to symbolize fertility?

... green is the colour of Venus, the Roman goddess of love and beauty?

... green was the favourite colour of George Washington, the first president of the United States?

... the green belt in judo symbolizes green trees? Just as a green tree is the tallest living thing, so should our pursuit of knowledge aim high, and we should keep the goal of achievement (the top of the tree) in high esteem.

... green has a toxic history? Some early green paints were so corrosive that they could burn canvas, paper and wood. Many green wallpapers and paints of the 18th and 19th centuries were made with arsenic, sometimes with fatal consequences. Environmentalists active in the early 1970s ‘reinvented’ green, however, making it today’s symbol of ecological purity.

... green plants used in interiors optically recede, helping to make a small space appear larger?

... green is used for night-vision goggles because the human eye can differentiate more shades of green than of other phosphorescent colours?

Goodbye black

Black was used for mourning by the Egyptians and the Romans, and today almost all countries associate black with death and mourning. Black also carries an implication of humility or secrecy. It is frequently associated with witchcraft.

Fashion victim

Black is the colour of authority and power. It is popular in fashion, because wearing black makes people appear thinner. Black also implies submission; an example is the black worn by priests to signify submission to God. Some fashion experts believe a woman in black suggests acquiescence to men. Black outfits can also be overpowering or make the wearer seem aloof or evil.

Black phrases

'Black humour' is morbid, unhealthy or gloomy humour. A 'black-hearted' person is evil. A 'black sheep' is an outcast. And a 'black day' is a bad day; 'black' preceding a day of the week – such as 'Black Tuesday' or 'Black Friday' – often symbolizes a tragic event.

How you make me feel

The colour black can make a person feel inconspicuous, can create a void in which to rest, and can evoke a mysterious sense of potential and possibility.

Turn out the light

Strictly speaking, black is not a colour but the absence of all colour. Black absorbs light and, with it, colour. White reveals and black conceals. Black is linked, therefore, to the unknown and the unseen.

l a c k

b

'Actually I don't remember being born, It must have happened during one of my black outs.'

Jim Morrison

Did you know that

... that the custom of wearing black during the period of mourning dates back at least to the Roman Empire, when the mourner wore a *toga pulla*, or 'dark toga', made of wool?

... that in some rural areas of Mexico, Portugal, Spain, Italy and Greece widows wear black for the rest of their lives?

... that in many cultures a black cat crossing one's path is considered bad luck? And that spotting a black cat in England means just the opposite?

... that black implies weight – that a black box appears to be heavier than a white one of the same size?

... that black tea accounts for over 90 per cent of the tea consumption in the Western world?

... that in China and Japan black is associated with honour and not with death?

... that a coal miner's disease caused by the frequent inhalation of coal dust is known as 'black lung'?

'Before, when I didn't know what colour to put down, I put down black. Black is a force: I depend on black to simplify the construction. Now I've given up blacks.'

Henri Matisse

Chapter three

Colour & Wellbeing

Healthcare

healing hues

Environmental psychologist Fiona de Vos discusses the increasingly prominent role of colour in healthcare interiors.

Author **Fiona de Vos**
Photography **Alexander van Berge, Rob Parrish and Derk Jan de Vries**

The addition of colour as a visual distraction or for purposes of orientation can have a positive influence in healthcare interiors, easing stress and improving the wellbeing of both patients and staff.

Many healthcare institutions are working to create healing environments, but most of their efforts are limited to beautifying buildings and gardens. Only rarely do they really investigate the needs of their users. Generally speaking, healthcare institutions are not places we enter for fun, even as visitors. A healing environment prevents unnecessary stress (such as problems caused by complicated signage, inconvenient parking facilities, sterile waiting rooms, long walking distances, a lack of accessible, pleasant outdoor spaces and so on) by minimizing 'mis-fits' between users and their environment, and by increasing the feeling of wellbeing for patients, staff and visitors.

When designing a hospital, there are many design-behaviour relationships to consider. For instance, what's the best way to maximize control and privacy for patients in an unfamiliar environment, to maximize efficiency for staff, to create a welcoming, supportive environment for visitors? The two most crucial aspects of all such relationships are visibility and proximity. A nurse (or nurses' station) visible from a patient's room provides a sense of safety. A visible day room is more likely to be inviting to patients than one that is hidden. Even when not at a great distance, amenities for staff (such as toilets and supply rooms) that are not in the immediate vicinity may pose a psychological problem for employees who have to 'abandon' their units – and their patients – to reach such amenities. A family room has to be very near to intensive care, allowing users to feel comfortable enough to leave the patient if needed. For appropriate use of colour in these environments, colours should be geared not only to the purpose of a room, but also to its size, light sources, materials and furniture. All these elements contribute to the overall image of a space. Colour can make a family room feel cold and distant or warm and comforting.

'They all look healthy this morning!'
When choosing colours, one should consider not only the potential aesthetic value, but also the secondary effects that might prevent the hospital from functioning well. The doctor who leaves →

Colour is used effectively for orientation at the KTHC. The graphics are designed by Studio Myerscough.

Oversized graphics that playfully refer to medical symbols enliven public spaces at the Kentish Town Health Centre in London.

the ward after his morning rounds, cheerfully remarking that his patients look healthy today, illustrates what the influence of colour can be in a hospital. Let's assume that in his department, sections of the walls in patient wards are painted orange. Even patients who are seriously ill may look healthy when bathed in the orange tint of such walls. As long as the doctor is aware of the cause of his patients' wholesome glow, the use of colour is not a threat to their health; it may even be of benefit to visitors, who surely like seeing their loved ones look less pale. By contrast, in an intensive care unit, emergency room or neonatology unit, where every second counts, the colour of the patient's face is an important indicator of his health. A green wall that makes the skin look extra pale and gives a false impression may lead to a fatal situation.

Research shows that colour can influence the way in which the temperature of a room is experienced. Painted in cool colours, the same space (heated or cooled to the same temperature) usually feels several degrees cooler than it does when painted in warm colours. Colour selection should be influenced by the function of a space, room or department, as well as by its location in the hospital. Spaces on the ground floor and the shaded side of a building, which are often darker and cooler, need bright, warm colours to compensate. Areas with more access to sunlight automatically feel warmer and more cheerful, so cooler tones could be considered here. A knowledge of colour is a useful and inexpensive tool to apply to examination rooms in hospitals, nursing homes, psychiatric institutions and the like, where it could benefit patients or clients who are – or believe they are – in an unpleasant or threatening situation. Surprisingly, it is precisely in these types of spaces that colour rarely is applied, even though it could greatly improve the welfare and wellbeing of users.

Reducing anxiety

Colour can help reduce the stress we typically experience when we enter a hospital. Today's normally dull and sterile healthcare environments heighten alienation, anxiety and the resultant

Artist Peter Struycken developed a varied but harmonious palette for the Martini Hospital in Groningen, the Netherlands. Rather than limiting the vivid use of colour to the walls, he included floors, cabinetry, furniture and doors.

Surprisingly, only one-fifth of the surfaces in the Martini Hospital are coloured, but despite the interior's predominantly white background, the overall impression is one of a cheery, colourful environment.

The accessibility and richness of colour provides distraction for patients

stress we feel when finding our way around the premises. A good example of how colour can change the image of a hospital is the Martini Hospital in Groningen, in the north of the Netherlands. The light, transparent building was designed by SEED architects in 2007. For the interior, visual artist Peter Struycken created a palette of 47 matching shades, ranging from strong (fuchsia, orange, green) to weak (grey, beige) and from light (pastels) to dark (purple, blue). From this palette, interior designer Bart Vos of Vos Interieur selected 18 colours, which he used in a playful manner throughout the hospital. Vos gave the walls, floors and fixed furniture in rooms and corridors highly diverse colour combinations without paying close attention to physical boundaries. A patient room for example, may have a pink wall, green cabinets and a yellow/grey floor. What's interesting to note is that while the hospital makes a colourful impression, colour appears on only 20 per cent of the surfaces; the rest are plain white. The lesson here is that you can create a colourful setting by applying colour to only a small percentage of the building.

Colour symbolism

The symbolism attached to colour varies from culture to culture. With regard to healthcare, in Western cultures white and 'hospital green' are considered sterile, whereas black and grey are →

associated with death and depression. Each country, each hospital and sometimes each department has its own culture: a subject worth investigating. A study of colour preceding the design of the Martini Hospital, for example, showed that the ochre-brown colour designated for the oncology department was too similar to the colour of the chemotherapy medicine, hence creating an unintended negative association. Bearing in mind that the colour of medication often changes over time, those responsible opted for a neutral colour. Colours like avocado and other green-yellow tones associated with nausea are also unsuitable for oncology units, as are bright warm hues like fire-engine red, which may provoke anxiety.

Orientation

When under stress, we perceive things differently; signage that may seem crystal clear under normal circumstances can be confusing to people under enormous stress. Helping patients and visitors to orientate themselves reinforces their sense of competence and control, increases independence and reduces unnecessary stress. Colour can make an important contribution to orientation in a hospital, but this tool is still greatly underutilized. Waiting rooms often look identical, causing patients or visitors who step out briefly to make a phone call or buy a snack to lose their way upon return. Without noticeable differences between rooms, people may end up in the wrong place without realizing it. Admittedly, colour is commonly used for signage, in the form of coloured stripes on the floor or coloured signs that lead to a particular department. A signage system that relies solely on colour, however, is difficult or impossible to follow for those with a form of colour blindness or for elderly people. In the Netherlands, approximately one in 12 men and one in 200 women suffer from some form of colour blindness. A far better idea is to combine colour with pictograms, patterns or tactile flooring.

Well-designed orientation is even more important when dealing with patients who have limited or poor vision. The vivid colours that highlight reception areas at the Rotterdam Eye Hospital illustrate the use of colour to assist in orientation. The original hospital – a tall, closed building designed in 1948 by Ad van der Steur – was renovated in 2005 by Marijke van der Wijst, who opted for a light, contemporary interior. For the reception areas, vibrant colour schemes featuring purple, bright green, light blue and apple green are combined with colourful horizontal patterns, generating a sense of unity and enhancing the visibility of the counters. Using unusual colour combinations, Van der Wijst conjured a 'grid of illusion': what you see is not always what you see. One objective of the renovation – a clean, uncluttered healthcare environment – was achieved with colours and patterns designed to discourage the use of walls as notice boards covered with announcements and stick-on notes. Five years after the renovation, the walls remain blank.

Distraction and calm

Colour also contributes to the interior of the Eye Hospital in the form of art. All pieces relate to sight in one way or another; they were selected for the hospital by art historian Ineke van Ginneke, who chose photographic portraits, symbolic graphic images and optical 'grids of illusions'. Colourful wall panels feature texts that refer to the word 'eye'. In one waiting room, 'I spy with my little eye . . .' is printed on a bright blue panel. Because all these works deal with the eye – with looking and seeing – the interior has a playful and accessible character, which satisfies one of the main requirements of the new design: the reduction of fear in patients.

It is precisely this accessibility and richness of colour that provides distraction for patients, assists in orientation and, in so doing, contributes to a reduction of stress and anxiety. In healthcare environments, actively providing positive distraction is important, because it helps to take the patient's mind off matters such as the potentially painful or uncomfortable procedure still to come. Obviously, visitors benefit as well.

Another prime example is the Kentish Town Health Centre (KTHC) in London, designed by Allford Hall Monaghan Morris Architects (AHMM). The hospital was envisioned as a vibrant building where health, art and community come together. The largely white, minimalist interior, which revolves around an internal 'street' and a spacious atrium-cum-lobby, is punctuated by Studio Myerscough's vivid, oversized murals, which feature graphic icons on the theme of health and body, such as a tooth, a thermometer and a footprint. The layered hand-painted graphics travel playfully across the triple-height walls, animating and connecting the rectilinear volumes. Colour is used effectively for orientation at the KTHC. A series of greens, selected for the hospital logo, relates to directional signage in circulation areas and bold floor numbering in the stairwell, while large black-and-white numerals on doors indicate room numbers. A green sign positioned above and perpendicular to each door projects from the surface, allowing the number to be distinguished from afar. Employees comment on the pride they feel to be working in a building that resembles an art gallery. Patients in the waiting room appear to be relaxed, and the level of aggression at reception has dropped noticeably in the new hospital.

Looking to the outdoors as a way of stress reduction, a natural approach to colour was implemented by EwingCole Architects at the new Cooper University Hospital in Camden, New Jersey. Focusing on the concept of the interior as an extension of exterior gardens, →

Oversized letters that climb the wall of the Rotterdam Eye Hospital refer to the well-known eye chart the optometrist asks you to read.

Bright wall panels at the Rotterdam Eye Hospital display Dutch sayings that refer to the eye.

the architects chose a palette of natural materials and plants to accent the largely calm, white indoor spaces. Warm natural hues found in stone paving, timber detailing and furniture – complemented by the vivid greens of bamboo, soothing sounds of nature and plentiful daylight – further the sense of a garden pavilion. Inspired by nature, the interior design calms patients and visitors with its feeling of serenity and familiarity.

Designing for the elderly

In designing for the elderly, other aspects of colour need consideration. A nursing home that proudly shows off living-room walls painted pale yellow – in an attempt to brighten the premises – should have done its homework better. Vision decreases with age, owing in part to the yellowing and darkening of the lens and cornea of the eye, and to the decreasing size of the pupil. A pale-yellow wall looks white to the elderly eye and goes unnoticed by many residents. The same applies to yellow-white signs that, by lack of contrast, remain a mystery to the elderly. Because adapting to different levels of light also becomes more difficult as we age, extreme contrasts between colours should be avoided. Transitions from light to dark in flooring or at thresholds can resemble holes underfoot and cause falls. (Look through your

Eye spy: at the Rotterdam Eye Hospital, works of art reflect the function of an institute devoted to seeing and looking.

All art pieces in the Rotterdam Eye Hospital relate to sight in one way or another.

eyelashes to get an indication of how a person with poor eyesight perceives abrupt changes in colour.) The finish of the floor is also important. A shiny surface (tiles, polished stone) suggests that the floor is wet, which may cause elderly residents to walk hesitantly, again increasing the risk of falling. Selecting colours meant to enhance the wellbeing of the elderly should be done with an eye to creating diversity and choice. Like everyone else, older people enjoy the option of choosing from various environments that suit different moods and backgrounds.

Designing for children

At the other end of the spectrum is interior design for children, which requires the creation of a cheerful, aesthetically pleasing environment that is inviting, soothing and interesting to kids of all ages, their families and staff. Many children's healthcare facilities use colour in the form of boldly coloured cartoons, pastel princesses and Disney figures on the walls. These may be suitable for young children but are too childish for teens, who tend to prefer subtler colour schemes. Young people need age-appropriate environments, because not only colour preferences change with age, but also the need for privacy (teens), for distraction (from toys to computers), and for interiors with relevant dimensions. Designers should listen to children (of all ages) to discover their preferences. Interviewing members of focus groups and asking them to make drawings are effective ways of finding out what children want. Studies have shown that reactions to colour tend to wane with time, however. This inconsistency – which may mean that, once applied, a colour fails to produce the desired effect – suggests the importance of using a range of colours to hold the interest of both young and old.

Studies clearly show that the impact of colour obeys few universal laws. The symbolism involved is determined largely by culture, and perception is affected by individual characteristics such as age, gender and colour blindness; social factors like fashion; and situational factors like form, lighting and environment. It is essential, therefore, to examine not only who will use a space but also when and under what circumstances. What is the function of the room? For whom is it intended? Is colour used purely decoratively, or is its main purpose functional (orientation)? Where is the space situated in the building? What about daylight? These questions need to be posed even when designing spaces bereft of colour. Too often in healthcare the use of colour is excluded, unfortunately and unfairly, when it could add so much value.

Food

black Stories

De Culinaire Werkplaats combine colour and cuisine to persuade diners to take responsibility for what they put on their plates.

Photography Courtesy of De Culinaire Werkplaats

Literally dozens of kinds of black food – including seaweed, dried fruit, lentils and rice – feature in eat'inspirations, a title that encompasses new eating concepts designed by De Culinaire Werkplaats, an organization that wants to open our minds to food.

Rice, potatoes, sesame seeds, tomatoes, olives, carrots, capsicums and seaweed: what do they all have in common? Besides being of vegetal origin, each of these foods has a variety that's black. Yes, black.

Black foods are not something that many of us consciously think about serving, but it's surprising how many black ingredients are available. 'We've documented 56 black ingredients to date,' says Marjolein Wintjes, cofounder of design/food studio De Culinaire Werkplaats (The Culinary Workshop). 'Actually 60!' calls partner Eric Meursing, hard at work in the open kitchen. Black walnuts and tonka beans are the latest additions to their list. 'Black' is one of the signature themes developed by the duo, whose Amsterdam-based outfit devises new eating concepts – eat'inspirations – designed to prompt diners to eat more consciously and more curiously. 'We use food as a material to tell stories and to encourage people to think about what they put on their plates. We want to inspire diners to set out on their own culinary adventure,' continues Wintjes. 'Black foods are used to trigger a narrative or a concept. It's easier to start a conversation with a black carrot than with an orange one.'

De Culinaire Werkplaats – part design studio, part vegetarian restaurant/workshop/store – was established in 2008 by Wintjes, who has a background in social sciences and visual arts, and Meursing, who studied to be a product designer and professional chef. Their work explores the food of the future; their ambition is to provoke diners to think seriously about what they're putting in their mouths. They use no meat or fish, which emphasizes the message that vegetables claim centre stage in their dishes. The message also encourages broader thinking on the use of seasonal, organic and fair-trade ingredients; on increased consideration for animal welfare; and on support for local, small-scale food producers.

Eat colour, feel great

To shake up diners' palates, Wintjes and Meursing aim for the stomach through the eyes and the emotions. It's here that wellbeing and colour play

A simple egg boiled in a pot with black rice and spices is transformed into a marbled treat.

'Each of our concepts makes you look differently at food and at eating'

Visitors to De Culinaire Werkplaats, a studio-restaurant-store combination in Amsterdam, can feast on nibbles in black, like this dish made of apple and black quinoa delicately wrapped in an edible 'paper' of black prunes.

major roles. Their Fresh Colour project views colours as sources of energy that influence human wellbeing. They believe that certain colours found in food correspond to particular traits, which they refer to as 'source' (red), 'focus' (green), 'radiant' (orange), 'larky' (yellow), 'inquisitive (purple), 'enlightenment' (white) and 'character' (black). For example, a green pesto made from walnuts ('brain food') furthers concentration, whereas a red tomato *sambal* encourages a sense of grounding.

For themes related to edible fashion, the studio is also developing a series of edible papers made from agar combined with locally sourced vegetables and fruits. When compressed into flat sheets, these ingredients produce exquisite colours. It's the black foods, however, that seem to shout the duo's message the loudest.

No lack of black

Hanging on the walls of De Culinaire Werkplaats are bags of black ingredients for sale. Shoppers find black quinoa, black salt, black sesame seeds and →

A hollowed-out heirloom potato (*vitelotte noir* or *truffe de Chine*) with dark violet flesh forms a striking shell that begs to be filled with yellow curry foam.

black lentils. The black salt, which hails from Hawaii, is the only ingredient here that doesn't start off black: it's coloured using charcoal.

Where did the fascination with black foods begin? 'When we first presented our design studio in 2008 at a festival in Amsterdam, we needed an inspirational concept that would express our ideas, and we it found in black,' explains Wintjes, who also has a strong affinity for black clothing. Since then, black has become the studio's signature concept, so to speak. Even though the culinary designers' themes have varied from honesty to water to flowers, each has included a black ingredient. When juxtaposed with black foods, the colours of other ingredients are accentuated; a plate of black rice, for instance, is a perfect backdrop – and highlights the vibrancy – of edible flowers, such as orange violets. Black crisps, initially created for a Dutch event known as the 'Black Market', are made in the ordinary way from a blackish-blue variety of potato. The process highlights the unusual colour and beauty of the swarthy spud. For a concept addressing honesty, black fair-trade ingredients were used to convey the message. The studio's research on the subject revealed a preference for black foods in certain health-conscious communities in the USA and Japan, where people appreciate the high levels of antioxidants in darker diets.

Technically, black foods are not 100 per cent black. Virtually all contain other colours: examples are blue-black corn and berries, purple-black potatoes, brown-black mushrooms and chocolate, and red-black bell peppers. Because black food may be mistaken for burnt fare, and because black is a funerary colour in Western culture, the associations aren't always positive. So how do diners react when served a meal made with only black ingredients – when they're given black *pappadums*, roasted black potatoes, black-mushroom croquettes and a variety of black lettuce? Wintjes recalls people giggling nervously and wondering whether the food was burnt. 'Others spontaneously mention all the black ingredients they can think of and suddenly realize they know →

Black comeback: like black potatoes, black carrots contain anthocyanins, dark pigments that double as powerful antioxidants, making them a delight for both the dinner plate and human health.

An inspirational image of a close-up of dried food.

'It's easier to start a conversation with a black carrot than with an orange one'

hardly any. People definitely show interest when, for instance, we serve spring rolls made with black-rice dough. A normal spring roll gets some attention, but a black spring roll gets all the attention. People start asking questions.'

Sourcing black foods for the restaurant remains an adventure. Certain ingredients are imported by the studio itself (lentils, rice, quinoa); others are bought directly from local farmers (potatoes, carrots); and the remainder come from specialty shops, such as Asian or Middle-Eastern supermarkets.

In today's climate, with the importance and future of the food industry such a hot topic, De Culinaire Werkplaats takes a unique stance. 'Although we can't predict the future, when we consider the development of food trends in coming years, Eric and I think that fish and meat will become less prominent,' says Wintjes. 'Reading this, a lot of people will think: oh, no, I'm going to have a hole on my plate staring up at me! But we see this hole as an opening, not a void. Inspired by this opportunity, we're using black foods to support an eating concept with a focus on trend watching – to show how exciting a black hole can be. Each of our concepts makes you look differently at food and at eating. Our projects ask you to view the world from a fresh perspective.'

Cooked black beluga lentils have the shiny appearance of the black food that shares their name: caviar.

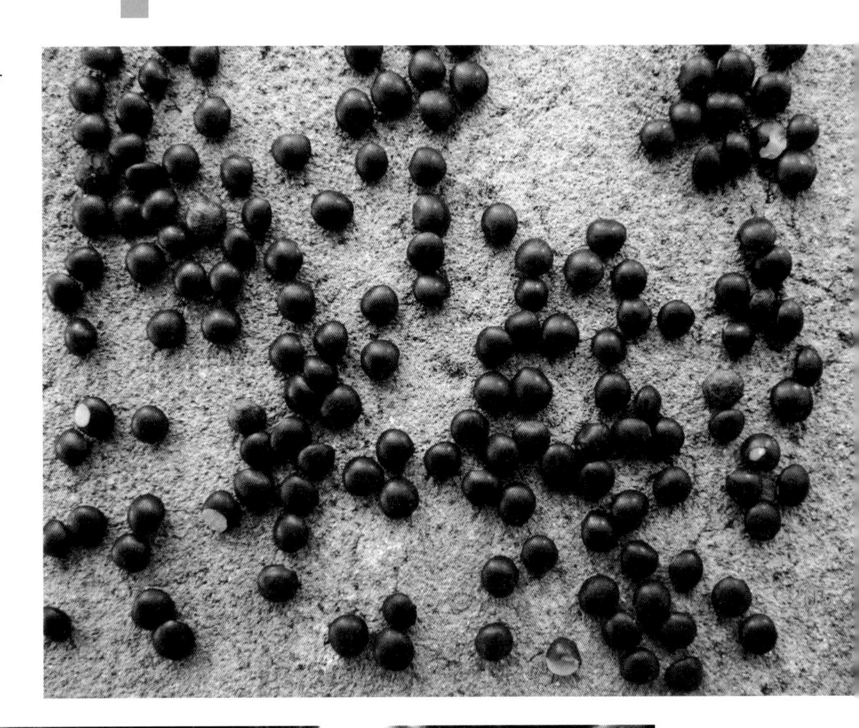

Plump, glistening blackberries are a commonly recognized and well-loved black food.

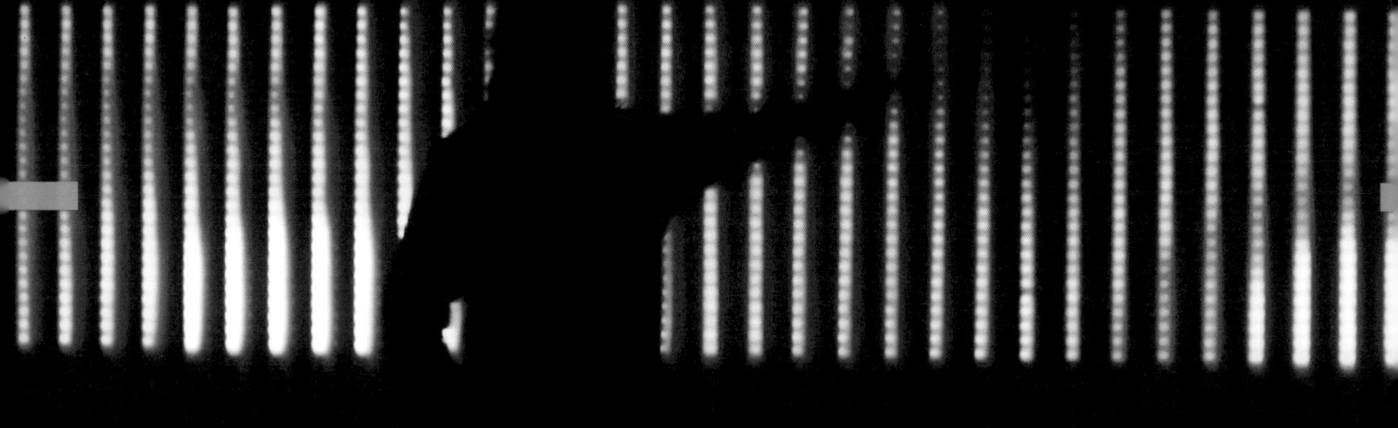

A coloured LED installation on the 24-m-long Moodwall in Amsterdam reacts to passers-by as they walk through a pedestrian tunnel and creates a 'presence' intended to improve public safety.

Seeing Sound, Smelling Space

Dutch author and scientific researcher Cretien van Campen explores subconsciousness to unravel mysteries behind the sensation of colour.

Author **Cretien van Campen**
Photography **Jasper Klinkhamer, Erik Krikortz, Åsa Lundén and Marcia Smilack**

What colour does to us goes largely unnoticed. Most brain processes occur outside our awareness, and what we discern is the tip of the iceberg. We become aware of perceptions, for instance, when we note that a landscape consists of a range of green shades. Subconsciously, or below the water line, is the bulk of the iceberg, consisting of the various emotions and behaviours that shape and steer our experiences and conduct.[1]

It's a wonder at times how, when riding a bicycle or driving a car, one manages to stay on the road even as the mind strays towards matters of work or family. Dutch psychologist Ap Dijksterhuis demonstrated that the greatest part of our behaviour by far, perhaps as much as 99 per cent,[2] is a result of unconscious decisions, and that we consciously control just a small part of our behaviour. For example, a certain decision is made – a right turn, say – and the body obeys that decision by making the hand turn the steering wheel to the right. Yet how the body subsequently manages to take that turn, usually without hitting the kerb or colliding with other drivers, is a subconscious process. The driver never needs to think about the degree of the curve of the turn; the action just happens by itself. In fact, things may well go wrong if he or she starts thinking about it.

Usually, we do perceive quite consciously the red, orange and green traffic lights, which prompt our decision to either stop or continue. Many other colours go unnoticed, however, even though our brain will have registered them. Lines on the road, for example: were they white? Was the road black or brown? Trees lining the road: was their bark mossy green? And the jay that flapped from tree to tree: were its wing feathers cobalt blue or turquoise? Even though generally these colours aren't perceived, they do influence our behaviour.

The conscious perception of colour, the registration of how light reflections in our environment differ in tone, the identification of these differences by applying the names of colours – all this represents just 1 per cent of the colour-processing that goes on in the brain. The remaining 99 per cent, which occurs without our awareness, directs a wide range of behaviours and emotions. The larger percentage is known as 'colour intuition', which is defined as the array of subconscious colour experiences and associations that govern people's feelings and behaviour.

As the definition indicates, colour intuition is a process that occurs largely subconsciously, although this does not apply to the consequences. Intuitions can guide people, prompting them to view a sunset at sea or a beautiful painting in a museum, or to move towards an attractive design in a shop. These people are fully aware, however, of the consequences. Suddenly they find themselves enjoying the sunset, admiring the painting or standing at the counter, holding the object, even though they had no intention of doing so beforehand. (Of course, they may have chosen deliberately to do any of the above, which would make the action a conscious decision rather than a matter of intuition.)

Hearing, smelling, tasting and touching colours

Starting to wonder what colour does to us? Particularly that 99 per cent of the processing of which we are unaware? Besides resulting in the conscious registration of colour-tone differences in the rear parts of the brain devoted to colour perception, optical stimuli appear to trigger other areas of the brain. Brain scans show that such stimuli can affect rather unexpected areas, such as those assigned to hearing, smelling and touching.[3]

The scans referred to here were performed on a small group of individuals with special perceptual abilities, such as the perception of sounds or music as colours. A small part of the human population, roughly one in 20, experiences these remarkable colour sensations, which for most people remain vague, implicit or subconscious.[4] People that have this exceptional ability are known as 'synaesthetes'. Artist and synaesthete David Hockney describes his synaesthetic experiences as follows: 'I find that visual equivalents for music reveal themselves. In Ravel, certain passages seem to me all blue and green, and certain shapes begin to suggest themselves almost naturally.'[5]

The reason for discussing colour perception by synaesthetes is that they perceive consciously what remains subconscious to others. An ingenious

Emotional Cities is an art project that invites people living in cities around the world to rate (online) how they're feeling. They base their evaluations on a scale of seven levels, and colours are used to represent the results.

The median result – which indicates the current emotional state of a particular city taking part in Emotional Cities – appears in the form of a coloured light installation publicly displayed in the relevant city.

Many synaesthetic perceptions involve colour: the dark-brown sound of a cello or the cobalt taste of honey

experiment by British psychologist Jamie Ward and British artist Samantha Moore showed that people without this ability unwittingly select combinations of abstract images and musical fragments that synaesthetes experience consciously.[6]

Colour perception is not just an aspect of vision. Scientific research demonstrates that colour also plays a role in hearing, taste, smell and other sensations. Phenomena such as hearing colour in music and feeling colour in skin stimuli are referred to as 'synaesthesia': *syn* means 'together' and *aesthesia* means 'sensation'. In neural synaesthesia, different neuroreceptors in the brain (those of vision, taste, smell, et cetera) collaborate in a particular way to produce these unusual sensations. In the brains of persons with synaesthetic abilities, the neural connections between sensory areas are stronger than those commonly found. Many synaesthetic perceptions involve colour: the dark-brown sound of a cello, the cobalt taste of honey, the deep-red smell of fish.

Apart from a small group of people with neural synaesthesia, who clearly perceive non-optical stimuli – musical tones as colours, for instance – a form of emotional synaesthesia is found in a large group of people.[7] The latter connect feelings and emotional states to sensory functions such as vision, hearing, taste and smell. These feelings or emotions often take shape in a sensory perception.[8] Or, as artist Wassily Kandinsky wrote: 'Represented in the world of music, light blue resembles a flute, dark blue is akin to a cello, while the deeper and darker shades of blue approach the wonderful sounds of the contrabass.'[9]

How synaesthetes colour their world

Synaesthetes use their synaesthetic perception of the world as a guide through life, as something they cherish and cannot imagine living without.[10] Synaesthetes' blogs, for example, describe the pleasure synaesthesia adds to their lives. The condition enhances and literally gives colour to their lives.[11]

In contrast to most people, synaesthetes experience colour intuition consciously. Interviews with synaesthetes provide a glimpse, →

At the moment when the image sparks music in her head, she takes a picture

therefore, into how the brain deals with colour in relation to senses such as hearing, taste, smell and touch. The following anecdotes demonstrate how colours guide synaesthetes through daily life.

Marcia Smilack is an artist living on Martha's Vineyard, an island just off the coast of Massachusetts. She clearly hears music when seeing images, and sees images when listening to music: 'When I look at this image, I hear a vibrato. How? From the shape of the bridge, by both the braided form and the indistinct or fuzzy edges. The colours influence the sound I hear because they are responsible for the instruments that might produce the sound of the vibrato – browns typically produce a lower-register sound like cello.'[12]

In the island harbour where the picture she refers to here was taken – and wherever special water reflections can be found: Amsterdam and Venice are her favourite places in Europe – Smilack photographs reflections on the water and prints them unedited as large-format photos. Her aim is to catch the perfect moment, and that moment arrives as soon as she hears music in the reflection. Smilack walks along the waterside, looking through the lens at the coloured movements in reflections on the water. At the moment when the image sparks music in her head, she takes a picture. Many artists would focus on the composition of colours and shapes in such reflections; Smilack is guided by the composition of the sounds that the colours and movements evoke in her mind.

Another synaesthete, Luxembourger Jasmin Sinha, sees numbers and letters in colour, as do many neural synaesthetes. As she goes about her daily life, these letters and numbers are a handy way to remember telephone numbers or names. Numbers and letters have fixed colours for Sinha: her 'A' is a sunny yellow and her '5' an alarm-red. She also has a form of emotional synaesthesia, which injects a sense of variability into the images and colours she sees. When facing difficult decisions with various options, she relies on the colour pictures that appear in her mind. Whereas most people might have 'a good feeling' about something, what appears on Sinha's internal screen is 'a good picture'.[13] In the darkness of her internal monitor, a transparent turquoise-coloured brick of glass may show up that she experiences as pleasant. Her feelings and emotions translate into coloured images that direct her decisions.

Colour in the environment

The preceding stories illustrate how synaesthetic colour perception can guide decision-making: how synaesthetes deliberately let their sense of colour guide their behaviour. What synaesthetes do *explicitly* occurs *implicitly* for the rest of us. So how can the perception of colour or colour intuition direct the behaviour and emotions of people in public space?

The following colour-perception projects implemented in public space show how the senses interact and how this interaction influences the experience of colour, as well as human behaviour.

The interactive colour installation Moodwall in Amsterdam, designed by media architecture collective Urban Alliance, demonstrates how colour in the environment can physically influence the feelings and behaviours of users.[14] The 24-m-long interactive Moodwall consists of 2,500 LEDs placed behind a corrugated semi-transparent wall, which lines a pedestrian underpass in a somewhat volatile urban neighbourhood. The wall 'greets' passers-by – via an integrated sensor system – with coloured lights or moving images. Currently, the actions of pedestrians and cyclists (the underpass is car-free) are translated into abstract patterns that 'accompany' passers-by as they move through the underpass. Moodwall was designed to increase the sense of security in this place: both on an individual basis and, more generally, throughout the neighbourhood.

Moodwall provides visual stimuli, mostly colour, which subconsciously affects human proprioception: the sense of the inner body. Passing cyclists and pedestrians are influenced without being aware of it. They feel more at ease and are perhaps amused by the intriguing colour patterns that walk or cycle along with them. Plans to show figurative images at a later date, like children's drawings or the work of local artists, will allow Moodwall to continue contributing to social cohesion. Local residents are pleased with the project, and over the

The Emotional Cities project in Stockholm features a coloured light installation in five connecting apartment buildings which can be seen from afar.

course of its twelve-month existence, the installation has not suffered from vandalism.[15] Both designers and municipal authorities expect it to keep enhancing the general sense of security and community in this area.

An entirely different project is the D-Tower in Doetinchem, a provincial town in the east of the Netherlands Rather than translating movement into colour, this project represents residents' moods. Visible from afar, like a lighthouse, the illuminated tower indicates how the people of Doetinchem are feeling. Visitors approaching the town know what they're in for. The tower is the collaborative effort of Dutch artist Q.S. Serafijn, architect Lars Spuybroek and the inhabitants of Doetinchem.[16] Every day the D-Tower computer measures which of four emotions features most prominently in residents' responses to an internet survey. At 8 p.m. each evening, the tower changes colour, or remains the same, for the next 24 hours: yellow stands for fear, green for hate, red for love and blue for happiness. So far the population has gone most often for blue or red (about 40 per cent each). Green dominates about 15 per cent of the time and yellow approximately 5 per cent. Incidentally, the survey steers clear of topical issues to concentrate on more timeless matters, such as love for people, animals or possessions; and fear of disaster or poverty.

The D-Tower is also a good example of emotional synaesthesia. The inhabitants of Doetinchem select colours that represent an average state of emotion. They cannot always explain their choices, which are the result of a subconscious process. Leaving aside the neural synaesthetes among them, they experience no conscious association between colour and emotion. Although both synaesthetes and non-synaesthetes intuit the relationship between colour and emotion, only synaesthetes consciously perceive such a relationship.

An international project resembling D-Tower is Emotional Cities (www.emotionalcities.com), which invites people worldwide to complete an online questionnaire that evaluates their emotional state. A colour code is used to represent the various emotions. The site's database continuously calculates the average values of cities and countries. Besides results posted online in the form of graphs, light installations set up in numerous places around the world reflect the local results in colour; one such installation is in Oslo.[17]

Findings emerging from projects like Moodwall, D-Tower and Emotional Cities are supported by evidence from scientific experiments that show how colour subconsciously influences human emotion and behaviour. For instance, businesspeople travelling by train feel more comfortable at stations painted with short-wavelength colours (blue), whereas tourists feel more at ease at stations with longer-wavelength colours (reds and yellows).[18] Blues are less stimulating and →

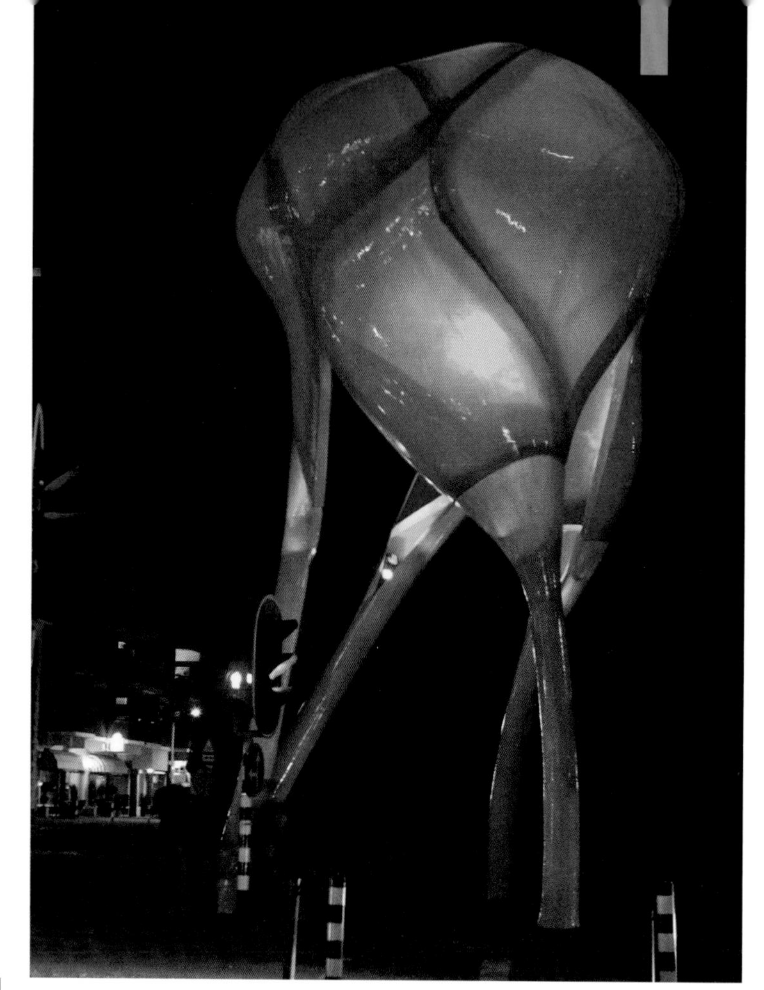

Fear, hate, love, happiness: every day the D-Tower in Doetinchem radiates the colour that best reflects how its residents are feeling. Participants respond daily to a specially developed online survey.

induce more calm, at stations and in other environments, such as hospital waiting rooms and teenagers' street hangouts.[19] In retail environments, if sensory stimuli such as sounds and smells harmonize with each other, a sense of balance and peace ensues.[20]

This evidence and that gathered from aforementioned projects show that the ambience of a particular setting is determined by how the senses work together. When senses clash, the ambience can become annoying to some, while others may perceive it as exciting or stimulating. Of course, personal preferences do vary. Youngsters seeking excitement and fun will avoid environments where sensory stimuli are entirely in harmony.[21]

Colour affects human behaviour, but not in a traditionally preconceived way. It is not the colour itself, but the way in which wavelengths of colour interact with other sensory stimuli in the environment, that subconsciously influences the human mind. Consequently, colour in the projects mentioned here is an expression or outcome of people's emotions, rather than the cause.

Naturally, the display of colour affects not only the immediate environment but also the emotions and behaviour of area residents and passers-by: consider how the streetscape is 'painted' by Moodwall, D-Tower and the coloured façade of an Emotional City. Neighbourhoods and other urban areas thus gain *couleur* locale by translating the population's subconscious behaviour, implicit feelings and moods into colour.

Observers of the future?

Colour is more than just the conscious registration of light waves in the brain; colour subconsciously influences our emotions and behaviour. Reports by synaesthetes demonstrate that colour also affects the way we hear, feel, taste and smell our environment. Their stories are complemented by extensive scientific literature that shows how the senses constantly influence one another at a subconscious level.[22] As people become more aware of how colour affects their behaviour and decisions – whether through interactive art projects or otherwise – they will also become more aware of the other sensory functions of colour. Our sense of colour is more than the perception of coloured light stimuli. The implication is that most people have the potential to become more or less aware of synaesthetic and multisensory perceptions that are, as yet, still immersed in the subconscious.[23] Because individuals differ in genetic synaesthetic ability, some will become more aware than others of synaesthetic qualities in the physical environment. Attentive and deliberate observation can help everyone, however. Most people find that a bass voice in a choir sounds darker than a soprano, but have you ever noticed whether the bass sounds dark purple or dark brown? Synaesthetes hear specific colours, which are easy for them to perceive. Their awareness of these experiences is a result of listening attentively and 'observing' the colours in their minds.

Designers and artists have a huge opportunity awaiting them: the exploration and utilization of the 99 per cent of subconscious colour intuition that influences colour perception and behaviour. As people become increasingly aware that their perception and sense of colour is shaped by sensory impressions other than sight, many will attempt to experience their environments in a more synaesthetic manner. Designers are advised to take into account the changing perceptions of users to their products and of visitors to their interiors and installations. Gradually, as the public environment becomes more infused by multimedia, human perception will attune itself to the relevant changes.

The growing number of people reporting synaesthetic perception indicates an increase in this type of awareness,[24] partly as a consequence of more frequent exposure to various forms of multimedia art. In addition to museum visitors, who are being introduced to synaesthetic art such as visual music and musical paintings,[25] the man on the street (and on the internet, of course) is being confronted on a more regular basis with multimedia and interactive environments that enhance his awareness of sensory interaction and cooperation. Colour is essential in museum art and urban projects. Colour is an international language through which people can share their emotions in an intuitive manner that may be nonverbal but is nonetheless widely understood. Observers of the future will, I expect, experience their physical, virtual and social environments much less in terms of the five classic senses (vision, hearing, smelling, taste and touch) and far more through sensory interaction in which the perception of colour may well prove to be the common language used to express their experiences.

FOOTNOTES

1. In the nineteenth century, the German philosopher-psychologist Gustav Fechner already claimed that our conscious behaviour and feelings are but the tip of an iceberg, and that the majority of physic life remains unconscious or invisible to us. G.T. Fechner (1860). *Elemente der Psychophysik*, Bd. II., p. 521.
2. A. Dijkstershuis (2007). *Het Slimme onbewuste. Denken met gevoel*. Amsterdam: Prometheus, p. 15.
3. R.E. Cytowic and D.M. Eagleman (2009). *Wednesday is indigo blue*. Cambridge (MA): MIT Press.
4. J. Simner et al. (2006). Synaesthesia: the prevalence of atypical cross-modal experiences. *Perception*, vol. 35, pp. 1024-1033.
5. R.E. Cytowic (2002). *Synaesthesia: a Union of the Senses*. 2nd edition. New York (NY): MIT Press, p. 312.
6. J. Ward et al. (2008). The aesthetic appeal of auditory-visual synaesthetic perceptions in people without synaesthesia. *Perception*, vol. 37, pp. 1285-1296.
7. H.M. Emrich (2009). Was ist Gefühlssynästhesie? In: J.R. Sinha (2009). *Synästhesie der Gefühle. Tagungsband zur Tagung Die fröhliche Sieben - Synästhesie, Personifikation und Identifikation*. Luxemburg: Synaisthesis, pp. 15-17.
8. Both neural and emotional synaesthesia occur in many guises. The American anthropologist Sean Day has spent more than a decade inventorying reports by synaesthetes. His website currently lists more than 60 types of synaesthesia, and it is striking how many of the reported types relate to colour. See http://home.comcast.net/sean.day/html/types.htm.
9. C. Söffing and H.M. Emrich (2009). Das Kandinsky-Projekt: Eine synästhetische Farblicht-Installation In: J.R. Sinha (2009). *Synästhesie der Gefühle. Tagungsband zur Tagung Die fröhliche Sieben - Synästhesie, Personifikation und Identifikation*. Luxemburg: Synaisthesis, p. 94.
10. C. van Campen (2007). The *Hidden Sense: Synesthesia in Art and Science*. Cambridge (MA): MIT Press.
11. Through the analysis of interviews with and accounts and reports by synaesthetes, the German anthropologist Alexandra Dittmar concludes that synaesthesia provides an 'orientation', comparable to how the left-right orientation is an obvious orientation in the Western world, but unknown to some other cultures. A. Dittmar (Ed.) (2009). *Synaesthesia: a 'golden thread' through life? Translation of Synästhesien: Roter Faden durchs Leben?* Essen: Die Blaue Eule.
12. C. van Campen (2007). p. 16, op. cit..
13. J.R. Sinha (2009). Entscheidungssynästhesieen. In: J.R. Sinha (2009). *Synästhesie der Gefühle. Tagungsband zur Tagung Die fröhliche Sieben - Synästhesie, Personifikation und Identifikation*. Luxemburg: Synaisthesis, pp. 59-70.
14. www.illuminate.nl
15. M. Eysink Smeets, K. van 't Hof and A. van der Hooft (2010). *Multisensory Safety, De zin van zintuigbeïnvloeding in de veiligheidszorg*. Amsterdam: Hogeschool InHolland.
16. www.d-toren.nl
17. www.emotionalcities.com
18. J.W.P. Peters (2008). *Meer licht op kleur?! Een onderzoek naar de invloed van kleur en licht op stationsbeleving van reizigers van de NS*. Twente: Universiteit Twente.
19. M. Eysink Smeets et al. (2010). op. cit.
20. A.S. Mattila and J. Wirtz (2001). *Congruency of scent and music as a driver for in-store evaluations and behavior*. Journal of Retailing, 77, pp. 273-283.
21. M. Eysink Smeets et al. (2010). op. cit.
22. To get some idea of these fascinating experiments, see G.A. Calvert, C. Spence and B.E. Stein (ed.) (2004). *Handbook of Multisensory Perception*. Cambridge (MA): MIT Press.
23. C. van Campen (2009). *The Hidden Sense: On Becoming Aware of Synesthesia*. In: TECCOGS, vol. 1, pp. 1-13. http://www.pucsp.br/pos/tidd/teccogs/artigos/pdf/teccogs_edicao1_2009_artigo_CAMPEN.pdf
24. C. van Campen (2007). op. cit., Simner et al. (2006) op. cit.
25. Cf. K. von Maur (1999). *The Sound of Painting: Music in Modern Art*. Prestel; D. Daniels and S. Naumann . *See this sound*, Webarchiv des Ludwig Boltzmann-Instituts, Linz, http://beta.see-this-sound.at; and C. van Campen (2010). Visual Music and Musical Paintings. The Quest for Synesthesia in the Arts. In: F. Bacci and D. Melcher (2010). *Art and the Senses*. Oxford: Oxford University Press, pp. 481-498.

Wayfinding

bold Messages

Vivid colour and bold graphics help increase safety at a car park complex in Sydney.

Photography Courtesy of BrandCulture Australia

A system of punchy colours and oversized graphics was adopted to facilitate ease of orientation and navigation in the car park of the World Square complex in Sydney.

Chances are, at one time or another every driver who's ever ventured into a multistorey car park has experienced the frustration of getting lost in a warren of concrete or forgetting where the car is parked. It's for exactly this reason that branding agency BrandCulture was asked to devise a clear wayfinding system for World Square Car Park, an underground facility that integrates car parks belonging to the various developments of the World Square complex. This amalgamation, situated in central Sydney, required a scheme that would guarantee the motorist easy navigation and foolproof orientation. BrandCulture began by investigating the most common mistakes made in the design of multistorey car parks. 'Research indicated that pedestrians were too often left out of the car-park planning and design equation,' says creative director Stephen Minning. 'In particular, it was recognized that pedestrians often experience frustration trying to finding their way back to a car in a complex car park, or have trouble locating ticket machines.' Hence orientation – for both pedestrians and drivers – was the main issue. Minning mentions that many car parks also put visitors at risk by not indicating emergency exits and fire-extinguishing equipment appropriately.

The solution lay in the use of blocks of bright colour and bold graphics, visible from a considerable distance and at eye level for both seated drivers and standing pedestrians. Punchy, easy-to-remember colours are linked to functions and to the floors of the car park. Blue relates to circulation: vertical circulation for vehicles (up, down, exit) is marked on blue walls, and blue lines on floors – the driver's main visual connection – point out major circulation routes. Blue walls for lift lobbies aid pedestrian orientation. Keeping safety in mind, the designers used yellow for precautionary zones, such as areas with low ceilings, and red for walls accommodating emergency exits and extinguishers. Used in combination with colour, large playful icons communicating the various functions further facilitate orientation. Minning: 'We found that in a large and visually monotonous cark park everything seems far away, and identifying these destinations means they become psychologically closer.' Motorists are not likely to forget where they parked their cars here: bold identifiable colours have been used en masse to indicate each level. Oversized floor and aisle numbers help drive the message home. Now that the problem of locating the car (and not getting lost in the process) has been effectively resolved, perhaps BrandCulture has an ingenious suggestion for that other parking-related problem: how to find the misplaced parking ticket.

Dedicated colours communicate various car-park functions: blue for circulation, red for fire services and yellow for precautionary zones. A special colour has been used to designate each floor.

Supersized graphics corresponding to the eye level of both seated drivers and standing pedestrians are clearly visible from afar.

Roland Schimmel's works are a lesson in colour perception. Adorning the side of a house in Amsterdam, one of his afterimage paintings plays optical tricks on those passing by.

black Sun rising

After-images, sometimes called ghost images, are merely optical illusions. In the paintings of Roland Schimmel, however, they become art.

Author **Anneke Bokern**
Photography and computer stills **DMF, Paul Kerkhoffs, Gert Jan van Rooij and Winnie Teschmacher**

All eyes are drawn to a single black spot in Roland Schimmel's painting, *Black Sun* (2) (2009). As you gaze into the dark hole, colourful lights begin to dance across the canvas.

All colours produce afterimages in complementary colours, but black generates afterimages in all the colours of the rainbow.

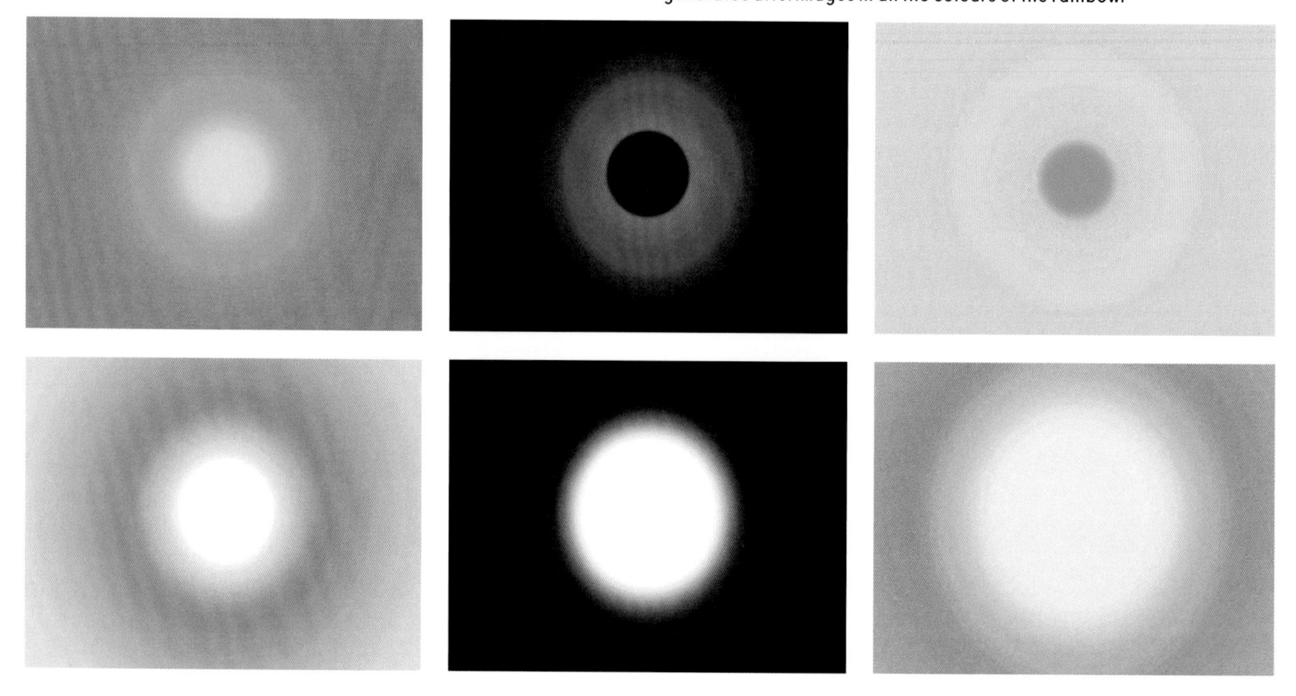

Dutch artist Roland Schimmel has been creating paintings and installations featuring after-images for nearly 35 years – and he's still fascinated by the phenomenon. 'Colour is a very physical thing, which can be perceived only by the senses,' he says. 'After-images, by contrast, are illusions. They are apparitions, chimeras produced by the human brain.'

At first sight, Schimmel's paintings, murals and installations are little more than white surfaces with a scattering of rather blurry, rainbow-like auras from which emerge big black dots. Upon closer inspection, though, Schimmel's black holes exert a magnetic attraction. The spectator's eye is drawn irresistibly to the circular shapes with their razor-sharp outlines and fathomless, intense blackness. When the eye finally breaks free, colourful circles begin a flashing dance across the canvas, blending with the spectral colour fields and making it nearly impossible to distinguish between painting and illusion.

'Staring at the black circle overstrains the eye. After-images are a bodily reaction to help the retina recover,' Schimmel explains. So far, so scientific. The fascinating thing about Schimmel's paintings, however, seems less a bodily reaction – referred to by the artist as 'a superficial phenomenon that even the simplest of minds experience' – than a time factor engrained in the word *after*-image and in the significance it holds for a painting. The works can't be grasped in the blink of an eye but must be viewed for several minutes before the after-image appears and completes the picture. Schimmel's clever use of colour allows his paintings to overcome a condition of static two-dimensionality and turn into dynamic objects. 'In my works, the viewer experiences the process of retinal recovery as the after-images keep →

'After-images are apparitions, chimeras produced by the human brain'

Roland Schimmel at work in the KetelFactory in Schiedam, the Netherlands.

The project *Duizend zonnen* at a residential building in Amsterdam.

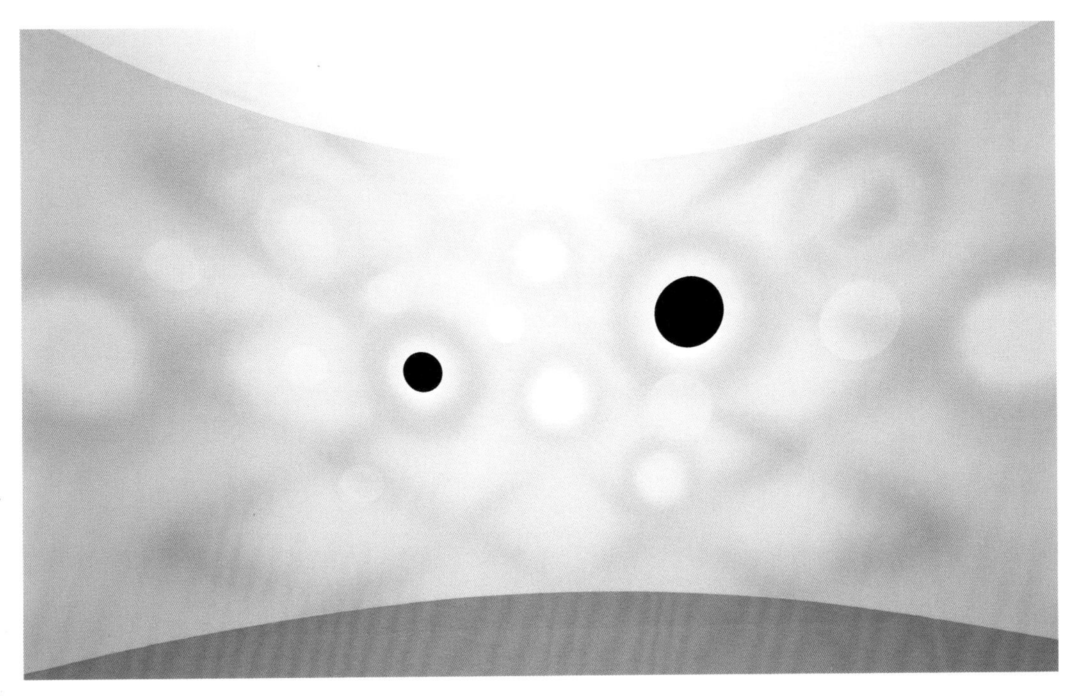

The installation *Psychoscope* at Culturgest Porto in 2007.

'My work isn't only about colours but also about illusion'

changing colour – and finally disappear,' he says. Paintings become moving images and, in turn, animated installations, while black – usually regarded as a non-colour – transforms into all the colours of the rainbow.

Airbrushed on canvas, the hazy spectral waves and orbs surrounding the black dots are nothing but our anticipation of the after-image our brains are about to produce. The nebulous presence of indistinct colour heightens the effect of the after-image and makes the visual riddle even more perplexing. 'My work isn't only about colours but also about illusion,' the artist says. In fact, his paintings represent Schimmel's decennia-long research into interaction between eye and brain, into the link between human perception and scientific explanation, and into the mystery of physical and phantom colours. After all, who can prove that the airbrushed colours on canvas are real and that the flashing after-images teasing the retina are not?

Schimmel calls his latest series of paintings, all of which feature the ecliptic black dots, *Black Sun Rising*. Black circles, however, haven't always been part of his work. A few years ago, his experimentation with shapes and backgrounds of various colours showed a keen interest in green on orange, which later evolved into black on orange. 'As I found out, the unique thing about black is that it produces after-images in all the colours of the rainbow. Other colours generate after-images in complementary colours only: orange produces a blue after-image, red results in green after-images, and so on. It may sound strange, but black offers the most diversity.' Which means that Schimmel's work challenges not only visual perception, notions of art, and definitions of 'real' and 'imaginary', but also the stereotypic theory of colour, defeating it with its own weapons.

The most prevalent type of colour blindness is the inability to differentiate between red and green. The reader without this deficiency can experience it to some degree by looking at the picture shown here.

Colour Blindness

When tints fade

While not yet a widespread trend, increasing awareness in design education and practice is considering 'colour blind' individuals.

Photography **Jeroen Bak, Courtesy of Miguel Neiva and Courtesy of AkzoNobel**

Strictly speaking, the term 'colour blind' is incorrect

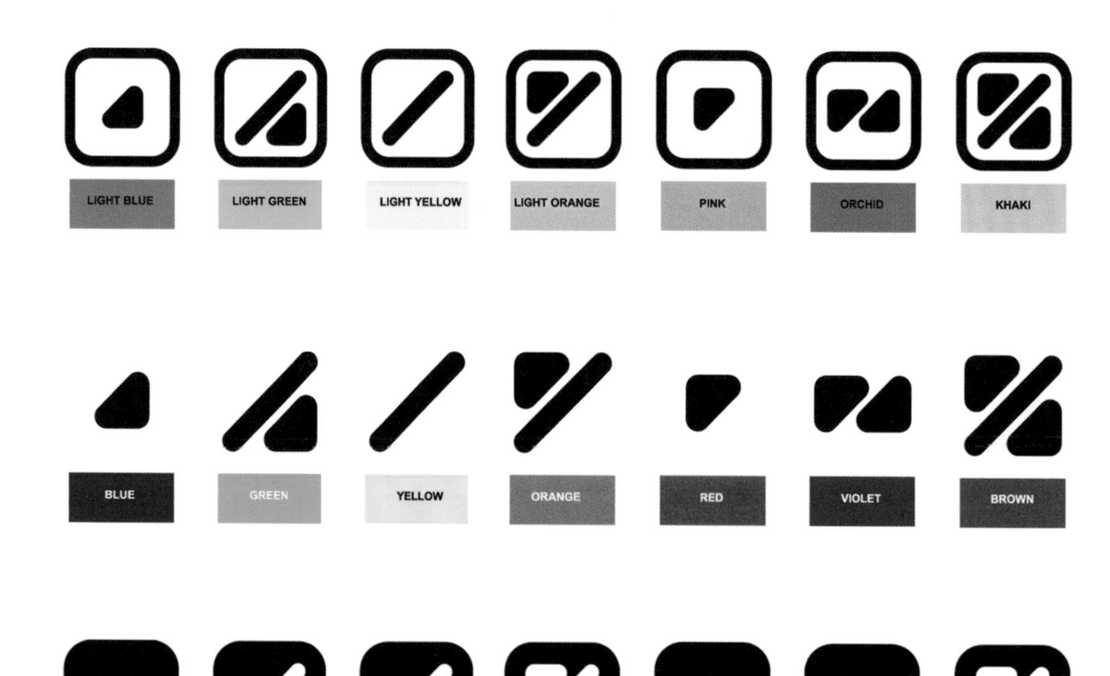

To provide colour-impaired consumers with a greater feeling of independence, to aid them in social situations requiring colour-related choices, and to minimize the sense of loss that accompanies poor colour recognition, Portuguese designer Miguel Neiva came up with the ColourAdd code.

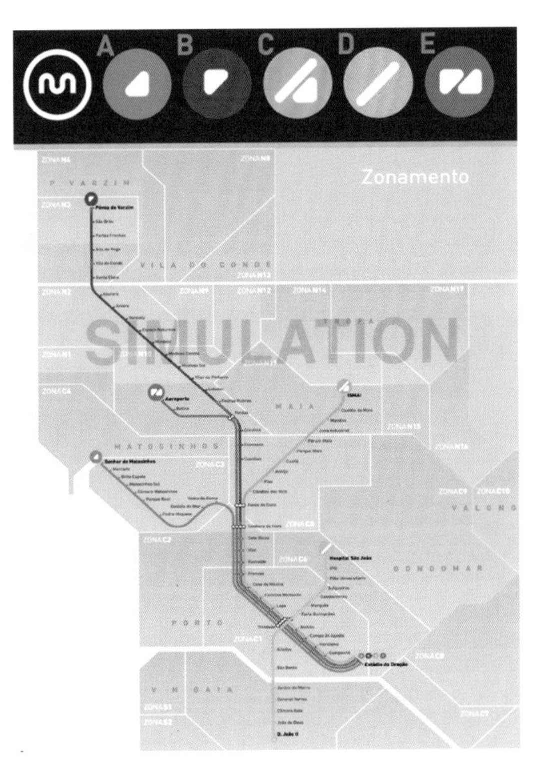

The ColourAdd system can be used to indicate the different colours of underground lines, as Neiva shows on a model plan of Metro do Porto in Portugal.

While the approach to colour in a design – be it that of a website or an interior – is influenced by factors ranging from cultural/client preferences to trends and context, it's safe to assume that colour in design is driven largely by aesthetics. But beyond its decorative or conceptual aspects, colour also plays a functional role. Think of maps, charts, signage, warning indicators, packaging and stationery. Do you think that colour blindness enters the equation when colours are being selected for such purposes? Chances are that it is not even considered.

The perception of colour in our surroundings differs for people affected with any form of colour vision deficiency, more commonly known as colour blindness or daltonism. Strictly speaking, the term 'colour blind' is incorrect: the condition is not about the inability to 'see' colour but about the inability to differentiate between colours. Approximately 8 per cent of European males and 0.5 per cent of females have this congenital deficiency, and some 99 per cent of the cases entail varying degrees of confusion between greens and reds. By contrast, confusion between blues and yellows is uncommon. The most acute and rarest form of colour deficiency is achromatopsia, which is characterized by vision only in black and white and shades of grey, along with sensitivity to daylight.

Colour confusion

What causes colour blindness? Donald McIntyre, author of *Colour Blindness: Causes and Effects*, explains: 'The human retina contains three classes of colour receptors called L, M and S. These are respectively sensitive to red, green and blue light. When the eye looks at a colour, the three classes of receptor respond to different degrees and then send signals to the brain. The brain interprets the relative strengths of the signals as a perception of colour.' According to McIntyre, the types of colour vision deficiency vary: 'Either one of the L or M receptors may be absent or the colour response of either the L or M receptors can be shifted. Since the brain requires all three signals for colour perception, a problem with one class of receptor will affect a whole range of perceived colours. The severity of colour vision deficiency varies from mild to severe; those missing the L (red) receptors have the most severe deficiency.'

To paint a picture of colour confusion, Daniel Flück, a Swiss IT education professional who calls himself 'red-blind', describes the world as he sees it. On his website, Colblindor.com, we read:

- Dark red/black: 'If I get an email with words highlighted in red, I can't see them.'
- Grass green/orange: 'I couldn't spot an orange lying in my lawn.'
- Leaf green/red: 'No red blossoms and no red apples in trees.'
- Bright green/yellow: 'I can't see if a banana is ripe or not.'
- Dark blue/violet: 'I'll never know what the difference is.'
- Cyan/grey: 'All shades of blue-green look truly colourless to me.'
- Skin colour: 'I can't see if a person looks ill or embarrassed.'
- Brown/green/red: 'Please, don't talk about red animals in the forest.'

The most problematic visuals for people with a colour vision deficiency include colour-coded diagrams such as public-transport maps, charts in documents and presentations, information graphics, and environmental signage. Problems arise when similar shades of the same colour are used, making it difficult for colour-impaired readers to match the colours in the legend with those in the graphic. Particularly hazardous are warning indicators, such as red warning signs viewed against a green backdrop (of trees or grass). Other frequent offenders are indicator lights or emergency buttons on electrical appliances or machinery, as well as those used to operate brake lights and rear lights on cars. Colour vision deficiencies can also vary with changes in →

lighting or material; a map that is difficult to read in a print version, for instance, may be perceived accurately on a computer screen.

To accommodate those with colour vision deficiencies, designers need to apply strategies other than colour coding or varying shades of colour to communicate a message or function. The use of text, patterns and/or icons can provide an additional level of information. Contrasts in tone and brightness can also help the viewer to differentiate between one colour and another. Often a large area of colour is preferable: big blocks of colour, for example, or wide rather than narrow lines. Before finalizing a pattern for a website, think again: particular combinations to avoid (owing to vibrations caused by the juxtaposition of these colours) include purples with reds and blues with pinks, especially when these shades have the same intensity.

Colour labelling

Shopping for clothes and matching one item with another is especially challenging for the colour impaired. One effective way to indicate the colour of a commercial product is to use text labelling. A simple listing of the colour combination of the pattern on a tie (red and grey, for example) helps immensely, as matching a tie to a shirt and jacket represents a major stumbling block for many colour-impaired individuals. After surveying 146 people with a colour vision deficiency, Portuguese designer Miguel Neiva discovered that 90 per cent needed to ask for assistance when shopping for clothes, and that 50 per cent felt embarrassed about potentially choosing the wrong colour combinations. With this in mind, Nciva developed a code to help the colour-impaired consumer to recognize and differentiate between colours. Basing his ColourAdd code on the CMYK system,

The same image shown with and without the Adobe Photoshop colour-blindness simulator.

Designers need strategies other than colour coding to communicate a message or function

he came up with a series of symbols, or icons, that can be 'mixed' to create a range of colour combinations. Instead of having to memorize a different symbol for each secondary or tertiary colour of the spectrum, the customer creates combinations derived from Neiva's five 'primary' icons: red, blue, yellow, white and black. Green is indicated by icons symbolizing yellow and blue, for instance; the addition of a white icon indicates light green. Although the code requires a basic understanding of colour combinations and although their number is limited, applications for colour labelling are diverse: from clothing tags, stationery items, paint tins and public-transport maps to the colour-selection charts used in software. The application of such a code to apparel would seem to necessitate an additional system aimed at matching various articles of clothing to create an attractive outfit.

Colour converters

There is an increasing awareness, although still in its early stages, in design education and practice of the need for inclusive design for the 'colour blind'. Tools such as websites and special software can convert coloured images to simulate what a colour-deficient viewer would perceive. From a business perspective – and particularly in male-dominated sectors – a company that is aware of colour deficiencies and is prepared to cater to those who have them can reach its entire target market without excluding anyone. Colour Blindness Converter (CBC) is a low-tech approach developed by coatings brand Sikkens in collaboration with Blind Color, a Dutch advisory/consultancy group. The CBC can be used by architects and designers at the beginning of a design process to gauge the impact that selected paints will have on red/green colour-deficient viewers (red/green being the most common deficiency). One side of the CBC allows designers to choose colours or colour combinations by scrolling through circular discs. On the opposite side, these are translated into the same colours as perceived by people with a mild or severe colour vision deficiency. On the back of the CBC, a graph of common paint colours recommends suitable – and identifies unsuitable – combinations: examples of taboos are lime green with orange and light grey with blue-green. 'This tool is both a reminder and a guide for architects who want to avoid the biggest traps in colour selection by considering people with colour blindness,' says André Koster, communications manager at Sikkens.

And, finally, architects and designers who are still unsure about their choice of colours or colourways can enlist the aid of a colour-blind friend, family member or colleague. Chances are they will be surprised to find how many people are more than willing to assist them.

The Portrait Machine Project by photographer Carlo Van de Roer explores the idea that the camera can provide an otherwise unseen insight into the relationship involving the subject, the photographer and the viewer.

Everything is Energy

Assuming colour is inseparable from the energy it produces, designers can use it to influence people and spaces.

Photography Carlo Van de Roer and Anouk de Kleermaeker

When the central area of the photograph is blue, the subject of the portrait radiates peace, tranquillity, contentment, tenderness, love and affection.

A person's aura is not static; it changes according to surroundings, health and state of mind

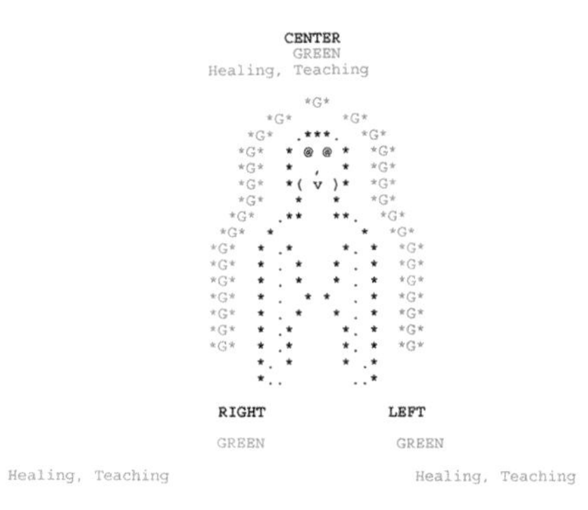

CENTER (EXPERIENCE) Color above subjects head.
Indicates what the subject is experiencing. It is the color that would best describe them.
GREEN --Healing, elasticity of will-- would best describe you. Green is perseverance and tenacity.
Persistence, self-assertion, obstinacy self-esteem, and teaching are the qualities most important to you.

RIGHT SIDE (EXPRESSION) Color on subjects right.
Indicates the personality that the subject projects outward and how other people see them..
Healing energy being expressed. an expression of firmness, of constancy, and resistance to change. --Elastic tension--.
Possession is regarded as increasing both security and self esteem. The person putting out this vibration is willing to work,to gain wealth in terms of educational, cultural, or physical attainments.

LEFT SIDE (FUTURE) Color on subjects left.
Indicates what the subject is creating for him/herself in the near future.
Green is a growth color, it brings spring to mind. Like the new grass popping up out of the dark soil, small leaves stretching out from the barren branch-ends, as the last days of winter slumber fade and the renewal of life begins.
Your future will be a growing time, a time for renewal, life springs forth. You are bringing in the healing energy to your life.

The Polaroid camera generates a printed 'colourscope' of the photographed person, which explains in words what is visible in the corresponding image.

Today, more than ever, we live in a wireless society in which invisible energy is used to transfer information. We have computers, printers, mobiles, GPS systems, televisions – the list goes on. Basically, we swim through fields of electro-magnetic energy every day. This is not a new concept, because eons before our techno-obsessed society became a reality people were wading through energy of a different sort: the energy inherent in all living things and in colours.

Consider for a moment that every living creature, as well as every surface marked by colour, possesses energy. The colour of this energy is expressed by its aura. All things – from humans to leaves to painted walls – radiate a field of energy. The colour of this energy can reveal information about the state of its host, and the energy of a colour or colours – of a space, an object, an article of clothing – can influence the energy of those who come in contact with it.

Colour of energy

A useful aspect of an aura is the information it contains about an object or a person. This information is decoded from the colour(s) and forms of an aura, each of which has a unique meaning. Although not visible to the naked eye, auras can be seen by those who are trained and open to seeing them – and, according to many, by children. Cheronne Jansen, a trained colour therapist practising in the Netherlands, advises clients by, among other things, connecting intuitively with their auras and chakras and 'reading' which colour(s) a client's energy needs. In the same way a psychiatrist deconstructs a patient's story, a colour therapist deconstructs the map of an individual's aura in an effort to restore the balance required for personal development and wellbeing.

A person's aura is not static; it changes according to surroundings, health and state of mind. Generally, the clearer the aura and the brighter the colours, the more positive the energy emanated. Illness and stress tend to weaken an aura. Hence clear, bright colours are Jansen's aim. 'Someone with an aura that looks like yellow light bulbs →

around the head is a person who thinks or worries a lot. Auras can indicate that someone is internally restless, that someone has a blockage; the aura shows where their energy is being directed. When someone is excited I see a lot of red around their head and shoulders. When the colour of an aura is pale, a person is obviously lacking that colour and its energy.' She interprets an aura according to where it appears on the body. 'Yellow as a garland around the head means creativity, but if it appears as bulbs, it indicates worries. A yellow glow around the belly, on the other hand, demonstrates strong willpower.' In effect, our auras make us open books for those who can read the colours of our soul – a rather daunting thought.

New Zealand-born photographer Carlo Van de Roer photographs auras for The Portrait Machine Project. He uses a special camera and a hand sensor, which is connected to the person being photographed. The sensor records the subject's electromagnetic field, as well as changes in temperature, static electricity and humidity in both the person and the environment. Interestingly, the contact points between the sensor and the subject's hand correspond to specific parts of the body, much like reflexology. The data measured appears as coloured fields surrounding the body, which are viewed on either a Polaroid photo or a computer screen. Eerily beautiful, the portraits are characterized by a coloured haze, sometimes vivid and multicoloured, sometimes so dark and subdued that it blankets the subject completely. 'I'm interested in photography that attempts to document the unseen,' says Van de Roer. 'A portrait is the result of a relationship involving the subject, the photographer and, ultimately, the viewer. The idea that a photograph can provide an otherwise unseen and accurate insight into that relationship is what started this project in 2008.'

How does Van de Roer choose his subjects? 'The tension between the different interpretations of the subject and my expectations is what interests me, so I've been photographing friends or people who are familiar to me.' The attitudes of his subjects vary widely, he says. 'Some come with a preconceived idea of what the interpretations should be; others do all sorts of things to try to manipulate the results.'

Energy of colour

From a design perspective, two main factors about colour should be considered. The first deals with an awareness of the messages conveyed by colours – and hence their energy. The psychology of colours is well documented; we know that colours possess meanings and communicate subliminal messages that have evolved through nature, science and bodily reactions to colour. In the words of colour therapist Sabine Rijssenbeek: 'Every colour has its own energy, its own story to tell. So if you use a colour in a design, you also use its energy. By becoming aware of the energy and meaning of each colour, you can proactively and intentionally use this knowledge in the design process.' It's no secret that red is an appetite stimulant and that blue has the opposite effect: think of how few blue foods occur naturally. Not surprising, then, that red is widely used for interiors and products that involve food and eating. Equally close to the body is clothing. 'When you wear coloured clothing next to your skin, the energy of the colours influences the energy field of your body. A red shirt, for example, draws energy up into the body to make a person more alert, more excited. By contrast, red socks drag energy down, grounding the wearer. Since each colour has a unique impact on the body, we can use colours as tools to recharge and rebalance our fields of energy.' Depending on the context, colours can be used to elicit a desired response or to have a positive effect on a person's energy.

Rijssenbeek also works with another form of colour therapy called Aura-Soma, which is based on over a hundred (108 at last count) coloured bottles in which oils float on water. Behind each bottle is a story that relates to a colour; →

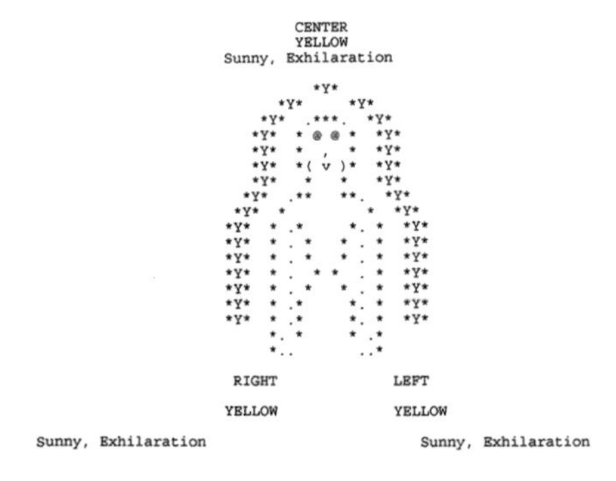

CENTER (EXPERIENCE) Color above subjects head.
Indicates what the subject is experiencing. It is the color that would best describe them.
Yellow corresponds symbolically to the welcome warmth of sunlight. Variability, expectancy, originality, smiling, and exhilaration are the qualities most important to you.

RIGHT SIDE (EXPRESSION) Color on subjects right.
Indicates the personality that the subject projects outward and how other people see them.
The world sees you as cheerful. Gold is the brightest color. You may find yourself the center of attention, with others revolving around you. Radiant, and expansive. You represent relaxation, a release from burdens, problems, harassment or restriction.Your energy shines from you like the warmth of the sun, giving happiness and joy to all who stand in the radiance of your smile, and you do smile a lot.

LEFT SIDE (FUTURE) Color on subjects left.
Indicates what the subject is creating for him/herself in the near future..
Your future is bound to be thought provoking. Like the rising sun, yellow brings warmth. Yellows are representative of the intellect. Each shade or tint of yellow expresses a type of function, ability, or expression of the intellect, from the craftiness of a mustard yellow, to the high thought of golden yellow. You approach the future with a sense of excitement and joy.

Our auras make us open books for those who can read the colours of our soul

Sabine Rijssenbeek's Aura-Soma therapy is based on over 100 bottles, each a different colour, from which the client makes a selection. The colours chosen, and the order in which they are selected, reveal insights into a person's state of being.

'Just as you can read the energy of a person, you can also read the energy of a place'

a combination of bottles makes the story more complex. A client chooses a number of bottles. The colours selected, and the order in which they are selected, reveal insights into a person's state of being. Like Jansen, Rijssenbeek uses colour to reflect a client's needs, to restore the body's natural balance and to improve wellbeing. 'The basic premise of the Aura-Soma Colour Therapy is that everything consists of energy – that everything is energy. Your body is energy, but so are your thoughts, your chairs and the colours around you,' says Rijssenbeek. 'Through your energy system, life energy called "chi" or "prana" flows through different energy centres called "chakras", each of which has its own energy, story and colour. The colours of the bottles are connected directly to the colours of the chakras. Your energy system tells you, through your choice of colours, which energy you need the most to bring balance into your life. Instead of using your overactive rational mind, colour therapy gives you a tool for using more of your intuition.'

Energy of spaces

The second factor to consider from a design perspective is the energy of a space. Rijssenbeek explains: 'Just as you can read the energy of a person, you can also read the energy of a place, a space or a building.'

Jansen agrees. 'A space has its own energy value. By playing with light, surroundings, colours, furniture and other objects, we can change the energy of a space. For instance, we can "heal" troubled spaces with poor fields of energy that are caused by energies that collide and are unable to flow.' She mentions the Chinese tradition of feng shui, which promotes the flow of positive energy. 'But it's also true,' she continues, 'that people entering a room change its energy, because their energies merge with the energy of the space.' She says a lot of what happens in a space has to do with the sort of energy people add to it.

Negative human energy is not necessarily damaging to the energy of a space, but the latter can have an adverse effect on the occupants. 'A room that feels stuffy affects the people who inhabit the space, such as those attending a crowded meeting. Having windows that open can restore the energy of the space. This is also true for cramped spaces and areas frequented by tired or stressed people. A meeting room will benefit from stimulating, refreshing colours. With enough light to encourage positive, uplifting energy, the occupants of the room will stay creative and alert.' What can we do to make sure a space retains its positive energy? To the best of your ability, Jansen suggests, fill the place with laughter, which invariably makes people feel good.'

By considering architecture or interior design from a holistic perspective – by looking at an integrated space consisting of layout, light, materials and details – designers can use colour and an understanding of environmental psychology to influence users' comfort and wellbeing. Examples plucked from research include the use of pink for calming aggression (pink has been used in the design of prisons) and blue for increasing productivity. Tempers become aroused more quickly in yellow surroundings. Jansen reminds us that objects are not excluded from this analysis: 'Chairs in red, black or yellow – each colour affects us in a different way. The warmth of a colour, the material used – even the shape of a chair – everything contributes to the impact on our energy system.'

At the end of the day, it's all about balance and harmony among people, spaces and objects. Taking energy and colour into consideration, designers can create spaces and objects with the potential to have a positive influence on people and vice versa. Food for thought – and a colourful meal at that.

With its characteristic, undulating, green-glass façade that references the River Seine, the DOCKS en Seine development, renovated by Jakob+MacFarlane, is dedicated to fashion and design.

Signage

green house

French designer Nicolas Vrignaud's flexible signage system for Paris' DOCKS en Seine complements the rhythm of the existing architecture.

Photography **Courtesy of Nicolas Vrignaud, Jakob+MacFarlane Architects and N. Borel**

The palette of greens used for signage at DOCKS en Seine maintains visual coherence with the new architectural intervention. Each floor is marked by a different shade of green, selected to complement the rawness of the concrete.

The chosen colours contrast beautifully with the rawness of the concrete

The signage system, with components that 'plug in' to the existing concrete structure, comprises a series of flexible billboards that can adapt to accommodate changing information.

With its characteristic, undulating, green-glass façade, the DOCKS en Seine development in Paris expresses one 'moment' along a promenade bordering the Seine. Located in the 13th district, the four-storey building renovated by Jakob + MacFarlane is dedicated to fashion and design. It houses a fashion school (L'Institut Français de la Mode), an exhibition/event space, offices, shops and restaurants. The refurbishment of this early-20th-century industrial warehouse incorporates a new façade whose green-steel framework and screen-printed glass has been 'plugged in' to the existing concrete structure. The particular shade of green references the colour of the river flowing by.

The building has a new signage system designed by Nicolas Vrignaud, in collaboration with Fanny Naranjo. The signage respects the existing architecture while also using it as support. Following the plug-in theme, Vrignaud created signs in the form of aluminium 'plugs', which are mounted on columns and beams and are grouped according to functions, such as circulation, facilities, shops and exits. 'We tried to prepare and to anticipate future needs, which is why we made the signage as "billboards" that can accommodate changing information rather than as panels with definitive graphics,' explains Vrignaud. By selecting a different palette of greens for each floor, the designers were able to maintain visual coherence between the signage and the new architecture. The chosen colours contrast beautifully with the rawness of the concrete. As they 'wander' along the promenade overlooking the river, the signage elements themselves become moments of colour, providing a human aspect that links the old industrial architecture to its fresh futuristic façade.

Oscar Diaz poetically addresses our senses and the passage of time with his self-printing Ink Calendar, which displays a different colour to indicate each month.

Design

time traveller

A calendar by Oscar Diaz features an expanding path of ink that highlights each day and month as seasons pass.

Photography Oscar Diaz

'The calendar not only signals time but also enhances the perception of time passing'

Thanks to capillary action, the ink moves across the calendar, filling the embossed numbers and automatically causing a new date to appear.

Pink October. A different colour of ink for each month illustrates how Diaz perceives a certain time of year in terms of weather and other seasonal phenomena.

Time literally travels through the Ink Calendar designed by Oscar Diaz. The calendar seems to update itself automatically as ink prints the number indicating each day of the month, precisely on schedule. Inspired by the capillary action of plants, which use the same method to draw water from the ground and into their stems, Diaz's calendar is made of absorbent paper, which soaks up ink, bit by bit, as the fluid travels slowly across the surface, filling each embossed number along the way. By gearing the constant speed at which ink is absorbed to the path it has to follow across the paper, Diaz has ensured that each day appears with precision.

Each month employs a different colour of ink. This relates to a 'colour temperature scale' that visualizes how people (in the northern hemisphere) perceive that particular month in terms of weather and other seasonal phenomena: blues illustrating the chill of winter progress into the fresh greens of spring, the heat-based hues of summer and, lastly, the deep earthy shades of autumn. This spectrum corresponds to a colour temperature standard called 'D65', which was devised to depict natural light. 'The calendar not only signals time but also enhances the perception of time passing,' explains Diaz. 'It relates to human sensations and impressions, not just to consecutive numbers. The aim of the project is to address the senses rather than the logical, conscious brain.'

Lighting

In the Mood

Philips' Ambient Experience combines colour, light, sound and image to create positive and personal influences on the experience of space.

Photography Courtesy of Philips and Frank Tielemans

The large-scale application of Ambient Experience inside the Frits Philips Concert Hall in Eindhoven enables the venue to be adapted to support the moods of specific types of events and audiences.

At citizenM Hotels, guests can customize the mood of the room in advance by choosing one of four settings that represent a range of reasons for the hotel stay. They can also select personal colours and light intensities by using the colour wheel on the Moodpad available in every room.

A patient arriving for an MRI scan at a hospital imaging suite fitted with Ambient Experience by Philips Design is in for a pleasant surprise. While waiting, patients can use a touchscreen to choose the atmosphere of their examination room: themes range from jungle and sky to mountains and underwater; special themes for children are featured as well. Upon entering the suite, the patient finds himself in a space awash with ambient, coloured LED lighting geared to the chosen theme, along with a simultaneously activated soundscape and visual projections on ceiling and walls. Patients can bring their own music to personalize the space further if desired. The multisensory Ambient Experience provides patients with a positive distraction that diverts their focus away from the discomfort or duration of the examination. Moreover, the integrated design of the room – with its characteristically rounded ceiling corners – tucks away storage and unsightly medical equipment, thus contributing to a calm, uncluttered environment to further ease patient anxiety and improve working conditions for staff. In the end, if patients are more relaxed, they're likely to be more compliant, which often means less sedation, fewer retakes and better-quality imaging. 'At Catharina Hospital in Eindhoven, 60 per cent of patients feel more comfortable in suites fitted with Ambient Experience,' says Jos Stuyfzand, the director of Ambient Experience Design, who equates happier patients with happier staff. According to Stuyfzand, the opportunity to choose from a range of atmospheres is a positive addition to the healthcare experience. 'Ambient Experience empowers patients; it allows them to personalize the space and to express themselves better.' Balancing patient needs with those of the clinical workflow, Philips designed light settings that change to optimize conditions for staff when required: during clinical procedures and, in particular, critical situations. Future healthcare developments of Ambient Experience will focus on healing environments, with special attention given to supporting the healing process in line with the body's circadian rhythms – to improve the quality of sleep, for instance.

Personalized and people-centric
Since its beginnings in healthcare in 2003, Philips' Ambient Experience has taken a 'people-centric' approach that was later translated to hotels and public spaces, using the concept of activation and personalization through image, sound, light and colour. The subtle integration of this technology into the interior has been made possible through the recent advancement of LEDs: 'With LEDs, we can create the specific colour of any particular spectrum using the RGB system. Changing the colour of the lights has become easier, and the lights are dimmable, making our goals achievable on a more affordable level,' Stuyfzand explains. Furthermore, coloured light can play a new role in changing the dynamics of architecture or interior, and in altering the perception of colour. Spaces fitted with Ambient Experience are custom-designed, therefore, to suit a specific function and to allow integration of the technology; a largely white background provides the best setting. 'Where we used to paint walls to give colour to a surface, we can now do that with light,' says Stuyfzand. 'It's a paradigm shift: where colour was once made visible with light, we now make colour *with* light!'

The personalization aspect of Ambient Experience rose to a new level when the technology was applied to citizenM. Designed by Concrete, citizenM is a budget-luxury hotel chain that aims to take the anonymity out of hotel visits. Each room at citizenM – currently consisting of two hotels in Amsterdam and one in Glasgow – features a Philips Moodpad, which allows guests →

'It's a paradigm shift: where colour was once made visible with light, we now make colour with light'

Integrated lighting in the shower and WC cylinders at citizenM replicates the colour of morning light and is activated by the alarm clock to help guests wake up just that little bit easier in the morning.

to regulate the atmosphere of the room according to their needs. An integrated system controls all the technology involved, from LED mood lighting, flatscreen TV and music right down to the soundtrack of the alarm clock. The Moodpad has a 'colour wheel' that enables the user to personalize the colour of the light by fine-tuning both hue and intensity. Guests making a reservation online can specify the purpose of their visit, which determines the initial mood of the room. For the duration of their stay, they can customize the interior accordingly, choosing from business (neutral), relaxation (green), romance (red) and party (pink). The alarm clock activates coloured light to help guests wake up in the morning: blinds, as well as translucent shower and WC 'cylinders' slowly radiate the soft blue light – a replication of natural morning light – that is most appropriate for the body clock at that time of day. The hotel's database stores the preferences of each guest for use during subsequent visits.

Ambient Experience takes into account the specific cultural and psychological meanings embedded in colours, images and sounds – whether in a hotel room or an examination suite – and allows for full personalization, in the form of choices offered to users. 'And if they don't need it,' says Stuyfzand, referring to citizenM, 'they can always switch it off.'

Public ambience

Ambient Experience can also be adapted to a more public context in which dynamic lighting is combined with sound and image to activate people and/or their surroundings. At Amsterdam Airport Schiphol, the subtle technology used in the Schiphol Innovative Gate keeps passengers company as they wait for their flights, while simultaneously supporting the brand identity of the airline using the gate. Illuminated with LEDs integrated into the custom-designed interior, the departure lounge emanates the corporate colour(s) of the airline: green in the prototypal gate that serves Cathay Pacific. Resembling animated magazines, video-screen billboards in the waiting area display flight details, destination-related

Technology keeps travellers company at the Schiphol Innovative Gate, where integrated lighting can be customized not only to communicate an airline's corporate colours but also to subtly alert passengers of their impending departure.

The subtle technology used in the Schiphol Innovative Gate keeps passengers company as they wait for their flights

The illuminated ceilings of the Frits Philips Concert Hall provide 'Intuitive orientation' to indicate circulation routes, while a central multimedia wall displays information alongside thematic animations.

tourist information and promotional airline videos. When it's time to board, a subtle change of lighting from warmer to cooler tones prepares passengers for the impending procedure. Thanks to its highly flexible technology, the Innovative Gate quickly adapts content and colours to the company in question, enabling virtually any airline to offer its passengers a customized experience.

On a larger scale, Ambient Experience has been part of the renovation of the Frits Philips Concert Hall in Eindhoven, a project designed in collaboration with Van Eijk & Van der Lubbe. The objective was to create a more theatrical experience. 'To start off, we went to different types of concerts – jazz, classical, contemporary and world music – and observed how people behaved before the concert, during the break and afterwards,' says Menno Dieperink, art director at Philips Design. Two requirements stood out: the need for an atmospheric experience to support the festive concert environment, and the need for improved orientation throughout the building. Consequently, the designers came up with different themes – incorporating projections and lighting, mostly in the foyers – each geared to a specific genre of music or a certain kind of event, as well as to the type of audience attending the function. During pop concerts, for example, high-contrast blue light generates a more dynamic atmosphere, whereas a warmer palette of reds and oranges complements the colours of instruments played in classical concerts. A large multimedia wall in the welcome area/lobby displays information alongside changing thematic animations. Denoting 'intuitive orientation', integrated LED lighting in the ceiling changes colour before the concert to indicate circulation routes leading to entrances and, during intermissions, to guide people to the bar. Like all Ambient Experience projects, here, too, installation has been tailored specifically to context, function and users. 'The environment changes constantly, but very subtly and intuitively. As a result, people become more animated and stimulated, making the environment a much more exciting arena for interaction.'

Group 1 is composed of warm hues (with a touch of yellow), high-value colours (light tints containing very little black) and medium-saturation shades.

Say it With Colour

There is far more to colour than meets the eye - it affects our total being.

Author Angela Wright
Photography Courtesy of Photographic Services/Shell International

After well over 2,000 years' exploration into the mysteries of colour, questions still remain about how it really works. However, in some respects more progress towards answering them was made in the twentieth century than in all the previous centuries combined. For example: How does colour influence mood and behaviour? Are there any universally attractive colours? Why do individuals respond differently to the same colour?

As I.C. McManus, Professor of Psychology at University College London observed, in 1995,

'Of course, physicists, biochemists, physiologists and neuroscientists now have an exquisitely sophisticated theory of how we see colour, but there the theories stop.' He goes on to say, 'Few colour scientists seem to have any theory of what colour is for and how it affects people beyond its mere perception ...'

Foreword to *The Beginner's Guide to Colour Psychology*
by Angela Wright
Kyle Cathie Publishing 1995

Colour affects

Colour is light, the only visible part of the electro-magnetic spectrum. Other radiations on the same spectrum include radio and TV waves, microwaves and X-rays. Perhaps because these wavelengths are invisible – whereas we can see colours all around us – most people tend to ignore the physiological effects of colour. We need not go into the widely documented visual process of perceiving colour here. What is perhaps less documented is which part of the brain is ultimately affected by the wavelengths of light that are colours, once they have been processed in the eye: it is the hypothalamus. This part of the brain governs our hormones and our endocrine system and, with the pituitary gland, activates the following functions:

- Water regulation
- Sleeping and behavioural patterns
- The balance of the autonomic nervous system
- Sexual and reproductive functions
- Metabolism
- Appetite
- Body temperature

The hypothalamus houses the body's biological clock.

This is the heart of colour psychology – the universal, psychophysical reaction. Of course, cultural influences and questions of age and gender do play a part, but in reality those factors are relatively superficial.

It has been demonstrated many times – notably in experiments carried out in the Soviet Union during the 1960s – that blind people can differentiate colours using their fingertips. In fact, everyone can feel the energies of different colours in this way, if blindfolded.

Clearly, there is far more to colour than meets the eye. It is a universal nonverbal language, which everyone instinctively 'speaks' and understands.

Nature uses colour as the main signalling system, and humanity has been acutely attuned to the messages contained in the colours of the natural world throughout evolution. In modern times, response to colour is on average little more than 20 per cent conscious, but it is still as powerful as ever – we are just less aware of its effect.

Colour is simply energy. There are no good or bad colours; it is all a matter of how they are used. We are rarely if ever confronted by one colour in isolation; it is a combination of colours that produce the response, and there are universally attractive colour combinations. Disharmony negates. For example, whether red is perceived as aggressive and demanding or as exhilarating and exciting is determined by how all the colours are combined (exactly like music).

Today, there is generally more acceptance of the concept of colour psychology than there was 25 years ago. It used to be said that response to colour is too subjective and too unpredictable to be taught. This is not so, and the underlying mathematical patterns that support colour harmony have been identified. Furthermore, the links between these patterns of colour and patterns of human behaviour are recognized. In 1984 the Wright Theory was formulated. The main tenets of the theory are:

- There are just four colour families, within which every colour naturally harmonizes with every other colour in the family →

Group 3 is the broadest palette to be found in colour space.

The colours in Group 4 are very dark, very light or very intense. Strong contrast – no mid-tones.

Colour is a universal nonverbal language, which everyone instinctively 'speaks' and understands

A person belonging to the Wright Theory's Colour Group 2 is calm, cool and collected. The code word for this group is 'Dreamlight'.

It's important to understand that 'achromatic' doesn't necessarily mean 'neutral'

– Colours from different families do not truly harmonize
– There are also four basic personality types
– Each personality type has a natural affinity with one colour family
– Each colour family expresses a personality type
This theory is the basis of the Colour Affects System, developed over the last twenty-five years. It has been tested empirically in application to design of all disciplines. In 1991, it came to the attention of world-class academics and was subjected to stringent scientific scrutiny, with consistently impressive results.

Colour groups/ personality types

Briefly, the colours in each group are:
– Group 1: Warm hues (with a touch of yellow), high value (light colours containing very little black) and medium saturation.
The Type 1 personality is known as 'Morninglight'. These people are warm and outgoing, light and ever youthful – fun. They are clever and communicate easily and freely, but hate to get bogged down in heavy academic issues.
– Group 2: Cool hues (containing blue), mid value (grey rather than black) and lower saturation.
The Type 2 personality is known as 'Dreamlight'. These people are cool, calm and collected. Quietly charming, they are diplomatic and sensitive; they do not put themselves forward.
– Group 3: Warm hues (more yellow than in Group 1). Can be high, mid or low value; can be high chroma. This is the broadest palette to be found in colour space.
The Type 3 personality is known as 'Firelight'. These people care deeply about humanity and are always curious to know how and why things are as they are and, if possible, how they can remedy problems.
– Group 4: Cold hues (containing blue), very high or very low value and very high chroma. These colours are very dark, very light or very intense. Strong contrast – no mid-tones.
The Type 4 personality is known as 'Starlight'. These people have great presence. They are quite contained and often very charismatic; they are most likely to be found at the top of any enterprise. Of course, everyone is unique. These brief descriptions are archetypal; there are as many variations as there are people. At the same time, there are millions of colours to express the diversity within each pattern. The underlying patterns are absolute.

Corporate use of colour

The environments we create for people to live in, to work in and to carry out a myriad of human activities are vital to our health and wellbeing, and colour schemes influence our mood and behaviour every waking moment, whether or not we are aware of it.

In practical terms, the Colour Affects System works as follows: just as any marketing team will look at a new proposition in terms of, say, animals (for example, 'tiger or elephant?') or cars (for example, 'Mercedes Benz, Ford or Ferrari?'), the Colour Affects System analyses it in terms of personality type. In interior design, this creates the ambience. Specific versions of each hue (red, blue, green, et cetera) are drawn from the colour group related to that type to evoke specific reactions in different areas. Thereafter, every shade, tone and tint is drawn from the same colour group, so harmony and psychological clarity are built in. Each colour group contains variations of all existing colours apart from pure black and pure white, which are cold colours and can seriously compromise warm tones. It is important to understand that 'achromatic' does not necessarily mean 'neutral'.

Far and away the most predominant personality type, worldwide, is Type 3 (Firelight) – and, scientifically, there are more Group 3 colours in colour space. Everywhere you look, you can see Group 3 hues, shades, tones and tints in action. Where the colours are all in harmony, they work extremely well; the trouble starts when someone lobs in a colour from a different group, usually prompted by an urge to jazz up a brand. Mixed messages emerge and the brand is compromised.

Let us examine two case studies.

It is important to understand that 'achromatic' does not necessarily mean 'neutral'

– Hotel Le Beauvallon, Sainte-Maxime, France

This magnificent hotel sits on an incline overlooking the Bay of Saint-Tropez. Opened in 1914, it is pure belle époque, and at that time it contributed significantly to the Cote d'Azur's burgeoning reputation as the place to be seen. Almost 100 years later, it was looking a little tired, and the present owners decided to restore it fully to its former glory in time for its centenary in 2014.

If a hotel is to be successful, it is vital to create the right ambience: a visitor's overall experience of his or her stay is greatly influenced by the 'vibe' of the hotel. People won't go back to a place in which they don't feel comfortable and – crucially – welcome.

The vital first decision to be made about the colour palette was to choose the colour group best able to capture the history, the grandeur and the elegance of this iconic hotel, while bringing it right up to date and – an important consideration for these owners – creating a family-friendly and unpretentious ambience. It was not a difficult decision, particularly since the building is surrounded by the glorious natural palette of Provence. The choice fell on Group 3. These colours are warm and rich; yet depending on how they are used, they can also be quirky, offbeat and even flamboyant, if required. Within the master palette, the particular hues for each area were selected to support the desired mood and behaviour – to put people in the right psychological mode. For example, the Beach Club restaurant and bar required an informal feel, best captured by the lighter, brighter end of the Group 3 palette, echoing the azure blue of the sea, the green of the abundant foliage and touches of golden yellows and orange. (Orange is always a good idea in a restaurant, as it stimulates the appetite.) For the luxurious pampering environment of the Luxe Spa, warm purples were recommended and, for the bedrooms, light, delicate, relaxing tints: a refreshing light warm green, touches of warm pink to promote sleep, light blue to calm the mind. The clients loved the palette and felt that it captured exactly what they were trying to achieve.

Shell offers an excellent example of the successful use of Group 3 colours.

Royal Dutch Shell Plc

One of the world's best-known examples of the successful use of Group 3 colours is Shell. The global group's legendary pecten logo contains warm yellow and red, and most people recognize the value of the pecten and of those particular colours.

Shell is one of the world's largest retailers. A few years ago, while redesigning its estate of service stations across the world, Shell researched how readily its forecourt shops made the brand recognizable to consumers. When respondents in four countries were asked which company's shop they were in, less than 10 per cent were aware that it was a Shell shop. The Colour Affects System was applied to raise awareness of the brand subliminally, since the logo was not displayed inside the shop. This entailed the careful application of more of Shell's corporate yellow to the retail interior, along with touches of corporate red, in a perfectly balanced way. Yellow is one of the four psychological primary colours, and used positively it can lift the spirits and increase self-esteem. Furthermore, it was essential to draw from Group 3 absolutely every hue, shade, tone and tint used in the interior – black, pure white and cold grey had to be removed. (In fact, black and warm yellow should never be used in combination in marketing, as the two together echo nature's own danger signal – think of wasps, tigers, poisonous toads and so on – and unconsciously evoke anxiety.)

When the project had been completed, the earlier research was repeated in the same four countries. This time, awareness of the brand averaged about 80 per cent, and customers felt that the environment was warmer and friendlier. Even the staff said the atmosphere was far more enjoyable to work in.

Come night-time, the radiance of Peter Kaschnig's Haus Blau drenched the surrounding garden in an eerie blue light.

Art

lost in blue

Austrian architect Peter Kaschnig painted a whole house blue to investigate the consequences of living in a totally monochromatic interior.

Author **Anneke Bokern**
Photography **Paul Ott**

Kaschnig's monochromatic paint job transformed an ordinary suburban house into a surreal sculpture.

'When I left the house, I kept seeing blue blotches everywhere'

'Blue is the invisible becoming visible. Blue has no dimensions. It is beyond the dimensions of which other colours partake,' artist Yves Klein wrote in 1957. In 2009 Austrian architect Peter Kaschnig attempted to prove this assertion with a large-scale experiment. Four weeks before its demolition date, he covered a condemned house in the town of Klagenfurt, Austria, in ultramarine paint, inside and out.

Kaschnig painted everything from roof and façades to furniture, flowerpots and toilet paper blue. Only the windowpanes remained free of paint, allowing natural light to enter the house. 'Before I started, it was a perfectly ordinary old house,' says Kaschnig. 'But painting everything blue suddenly made it special. Blue paint unified all materials and visual layers of the structure. Light changed, spaces were de-familiarized and the structure became unreal.'

To experience the effects of a monochromatic interior, Kaschnig repeatedly remained in the house for up to 12 hours. 'I chose ultramarine because of its lack of nuance and because it offers very little relief. My eyes looked for a point of rest but couldn't find one. I had no colour differences to focus on. The colour covered the visual and haptic characteristics of all materials. It hid any trace of use, making all objects passive,' Kaschnig recounts. 'Contrary to what one would expect, the rooms appeared smaller. The stairwell and the basement, in particular, were very oppressive. The ceiling was indistinguishable from the floor, producing a state of total disorientation and alienation. When I left the house, I kept seeing blue blotches everywhere.'

The house is gone, but Kaschnig can imagine taking the experiment even further. 'The project could be raised to another level by making the surroundings monochromatic as well. And a thick layer of snow would add a sense of natural monochromization.'

The interior of Haus Blau breathed an air of alienation, because everything was painted blue except the windowpanes.

About the Authors

Designer and consultant Hanneke Kamphuis focuses on designing prints and developing colour and material concepts for the retail industry. As a fashion graduate of the Arnhem Academy of Art, she currently lectures at several Dutch design academies.

Designer Hedwig van Onna develops colour concepts for interior design, healthcare and multisensory projects. As a design graduate of the Design Academy Eindhoven, Van Onna also teaches colour and visual-communication courses at various design schools in the Netherlands.

Architecture and design journalist Jeanne Tan was born in Malaysia, studied architecture in Australia and Sweden, and now calls Amsterdam home. She has contributed to major international design publications; her area of expertise covers culture, process and sustainability in design.

Anneke Bokern is a freelance writer specializing in architecture, design and art. Born in Frankfurt, Germany, she moved to Amsterdam in 2000. Her articles have appeared in various German and international magazines.

Cretien van Campen is a scientific researcher and the founder of Synesthetics Netherlands. As a psychologist and art historian, he explores the boundaries of perception in the arts and the sciences. As a social scientist, he is researching the state of health and happiness of the Dutch population for the Social and Cultural Planning Office.

A self-confessed colour addict, Leatrice Eiseman founded the Eiseman Center for Color Information and is executive director of the Pantone Color Institute. She is the author of seven books on colour and, as a colour specialist, provides expertise where colour choice is critical to the success of a product or an environment. She also teaches programmes that involve the psychology of colour and insights on colour trends and forecasting.

Ted Mininni is president and creative director of Design Force, Inc., a consultancy located in New Jersey. Mininni's expertise lies in connecting consumers to brands emotionally by creating compelling visual brand experiences with the dynamic use of brand identity and package structure. Design Force also specializes in the development of systems for package design.

Dr Sam Spurr is a designer, theorist and critic whose research focuses on the exploration of performance and architecture. Spurr is director of the Interior and Spatial Design Program at the University of Technology, Sydney.

Fiona de Vos is an environmental psychologist and a pioneer in healing environments. She lives and works in the Netherlands. She has worked as an independent consultant and researcher for the past 15 years, focusing on programming and evaluating healthcare, workplace and children's environments.

Angela Wright is the founder of Colour Affects, a London colour consultancy that has been applying colour psychology with great success since 1985. Her 1995 book, *The Beginner's Guide to Colour Psychology*, is in its seventh reprint.

Colour Hunting
How Colour Influences
What We Buy, Make and Feel

Publisher
Frame Publishers

Compiled by
Hanneke Kamphuis
Hedwig van Onna

Production
Marlous van Rossum-Willems

Author
Jeanne Tan

Contributing authors
Anneke Bokern, Cretien van Campen, Leatrice Eiseman, Ted Mininni, Sam Spurr, Fiona de Vos and Angela Wright

Graphic design
Mariëlle van Genderen
Adriaan Mellegers

Copy editing
InOtherWords (Donna de Vries-Hermansader and Gwendie Camp)

Prepress
Edward de Nijs

Printing
Ofset Yapimevi

Trade distribution USA and Canada
Consortium Book Sales & Distribution, LLC.
34 Thirteenth Avenue NE, Suite 101
Minneapolis, MN 55413-1007
T +1 612 746 2600
T +1 800 283 3572 (orders)
F +1 612 746 2606

Distribution rest of world
Frame Publishers
Laan der Hesperiden 68
1076 DX Amsterdam
The Netherlands
www.framemag.com
distribution@framemag.com

ISBN: 978-90-77174-27-2

The Koninklijke Bibliotheek lists this publication in the Nederlandse Bibliografie: detailed bibliographic information is available on the internet at http://picarta.pica.nl

Printed on acid-free paper produced from chlorine-free pulp. TCF ∞
Printed in Turkey

987654321